PENGU
NOBODY CAN

A writer of city life, Mayank Aust . . . . . usties out daily dispatches for *Hindustan Times*. He spends his time in bookshops and bylanes, observing every corner of the metropolis. Once a hotel steward, he is best known for his blog, The Delhi Walla, in which he details Delhi's lives and loves.

PRAISE FOR THE BOOK

'A deeply moving account of the lives, sufferings and routines of a dark segment of Delhi's society'—Ashok Vajpeyi

'A true picture of the enigmatic world of Delhi's red light area . . . he writes as his subjects' friend rather than a journalist'—*Tehelka*

'The question[s] of morality, religion and hypocrisy hang in the balance . . . one of the best non-fiction reads for this year'—*Sentinel*

'Graceful yet powerful'—*DNA*

'Soofi's writing is gripping, observational and intimate'—*Financial Express*

'A sensitive account . . . that reveals, among other things, how tenuous the lines can be between ostracism and social acceptance' —*Sunday Statesman*

'Soofi explores this half-hidden world with honesty . . . and is adept at navigating the shadows between the dark wretchedness and sunny familiarity of these women's lives'—*South China Morning Post*

'There's no proselytising in Soofi's narrative, no sensationalising of the profession, there is just a vivid documentation of his experiences'—*Mid Day*

Nobody can Love you more

*Life in Delhi's
Red Light District*

Mayank Austen Soofi

PENGUIN BOOKS
An imprint of Penguin Random House

PENGUIN BOOKS

USA | Canada | UK | Ireland | Australia
New Zealand | India | South Africa | China

Penguin Books is part of the Penguin Random House group of companies
whose addresses can be found at global.penguinrandomhouse.com

Published by Penguin Random House India Pvt. Ltd
4th Floor, Capital Tower 1, MG Road,
Gurugram 122 002, Haryana, India

Penguin
Random House
India

First published in Viking by Penguin Books India 2012
Published in Penguin Books 2014
This edition published 2019

ISBN 9780143422723

Book design by Solveig Bang
Typeset in Adobe Caslon Pro
Printed at Repro India Limited

www.penguin.co.in

MIX
Paper from
responsible sources
FSC® C047271

For
Sri Kshetrapal Singh and Srimati Pushpa Singh
and
Hazrat Nizamuddin Auliya

When I went to that house of pleasure
I didn't stay in the front rooms where they celebrate,
with some decorum, the accepted modes of love.

I went into the secret rooms
and lounged and lay on their beds.

Cavafy

Contents

I had gone too far

TAKE SUSHMA. No cataclysm ever disrupted the progression of her life. One day led to another. The years rolled by. Old acquaintances were left behind, new friends were made. Youth ended and middle age began. She put on weight. Disappointments came, and so did a few delights. Sushma is no extraordinary woman. She shivers in winter and catches fevers with the change of seasons. She buys vegetables in the evening and smokes 502 Pataka beedis while cooking. She makes love and makes money.

Sushma is forty-six or forty-seven—she isn't sure. She talks to me in Hindi but says she is a south Indian from Bangalore. 'Sushma' is a Hindu name but she is a Muslim. 'My real name . . .' she says. We are sitting in a dimly lit room in kotha number *teen sau* (300). It is late November and outside the sky is grey. She is wrapped in a shawl. 'What will you do with my real name?' she asks. I persist. 'Shireen,' she says. A beautiful name but she doesn't know what it means. 'Shireen', of Persian origin, means 'sweet'. When I try to imagine a woman called Shireen, I see a slim Parsi lady of fair complexion. Used to wearing finely embroidered *gara* saris, my Shireen must have received education from a private school in Ooty. She probably owns a summer house in London and an apartment in south Bombay. Born into an old-money family, she got married into another old-money family. The name 'Shireen' doesn't suit the person of Sushma. Sushma is a sex worker. Her rate is 150 rupees. After bargaining, it can come down to 120 rupees. A smart customer can bring it down further to 100 rupees.

'I never give my real name. No woman here ever does. Nobody knows our real names except maybe the kotha malik. If somebody asks, we give fictitious names. You never know . . . just in case something happens. What if word about you reaches your family? They don't know what we do, you know.'

Sushma's work begins a few hours after midnight. 'I don't like standing outside during the day. It's not something pleasant. Of course, if a customer climbs up the stairs, say, right now, and asks for me, I won't refuse.'

Otherwise, at 3 every morning Sushma walks down the twenty-seven stairs from the second-floor kotha to the covered walkway outside and there she stays till 7 a.m., looking for men. In these early morning hours, GB Road is visited by people whose jobs entail late-night shifts. Done with their work, these men—immigrants working as dhaba waiters, auto drivers, daily-wage labourers and rickshaw pullers—come to find solace in the flesh of women. 'In the morning, once I'm finished, I have chai in Shahganj, behind the kotha, and then I go up and sleep.'

At night, Sushma goes to sleep by 10. 'Fatima didi wakes me up at 2.30 in the morning. She keeps chai ready for me. I wash, get ready and go down.' Sushma does not dress in shining costumes. 'No *chamak dhamak* clothes. In the morning when I'm getting ready to go down, I put on a simple salwar suit. I believe that if you have to get a client, you will get him. Yes, but I make sure that my dress is clean.'

Sushma wears black-rimmed spectacles. As I ask her to show me the colour of her eyes, she takes off the glasses, bends towards me and opens her eyes wide. They seem black but the overhanging bulb gives off a faint glow and I cannot be sure. 'I never liked bright colours. As a child, I was drawn towards lighter shades like pale green, sky blue, soft pink and even navy blue. Back then I always wore a skirt and a blouse. The tailor would make middies for me. When I grew up, I started wearing salwar suits.'

A thick black thread is slung around Sushma's neck. It has a key that goes deep down into her cleavage. 'People keep asking what it is. I tell them it's a magic *chabbi* to ward off evil.' She pauses for effect. 'But it's just a joke,' she laughs. 'It's the key to my trunk. I will to lose it if I keep it somewhere else.'

The trunk is kept on the kotha's roof, under a tin shed serving as Sushma's home. In a manner of speaking, the trunk is her wardrobe, packed with twenty-three salwar suits and a dozen saris. 'I'm not used to saris. I find it difficult to walk down the stairs when I'm wearing one. Now when I think of it, Mummy would only wear saris. In the south, you don't see married women in salwar suits. Mummy died when I was in the seventh standard. I haven't forgotten her face. She looked lovely when she dressed in light yellow shades. She would never put on much make-up. I've taken after her.'

Early in the morning, while getting ready to find customers, Sushma lines her eyes with kajal. Like a married woman, she puts on a red Shilpa bindi on her forehead. Her cheeks are patted down with a smidgen of Fair & Lovely cream. Because it is winter, Sushma smooths the dryness of the skin with Pond's cold cream. The final addition is the light Coca-Cola-coloured Pond's lipstick. 'Look at my lips. They are dark brown, almost black. 'Four years ago I used a cheap lipstick. I was trying to save money, and look what that did to my lips. It seems sort of okay now. My lips were swollen and discoloured then—I had to go to a doctor. He said I must use only company*wali* lipstick.'

AT 3 A.M., THERE IS NO CERTAINTY of customers for middle-aged Sushma. 'Sometimes I get two. Sometimes four. Sometimes none.' She makes about Rs 5000 a month. 'Out of the 120 rupees I make from each customer, I give 70 rupees to Bhayya.' Bhayya, whom I know as Sabir Bhai, runs the kotha. 'That sum includes the rent, and the bill for water and electricity. I don't have to worry about these details once I've paid my share.'

Sushma's daily expenses add up to about 80 rupees. 'Look, in the morning before calling it a day, I have chai outside from a stall for 7 rupees, and *biskut* and *tambakoo* for 3 rupees. In the afternoon, I go to Shahganj to buy vegetables. Yesterday I spent 30 rupees on potatoes, tomatoes, garlic, ginger, onions, coriander leaves and green chillies. And then every day you discover that the cooking oil or something else is finished. A small salt packet costs 13 rupees!' Sushma has a savings account at the State Bank of India. When I ask how much money she has in there, she is evasive.

'Maybe two lakhs?' I say.

'Ah, listen to you! If I had that much, would I be here?' she laughs.

WHAT DOES A MAN SEE IN SUSHMA when he decides to spend his money to sleep with her? I search for clues. The grey strands of her hair are dyed orange with henna. Her eyebrows are sparse, almost absent. Her eyes have dark shadows underneath them. The bridge of her nose is almost flat, the nostrils spread wide. Faint lines of ageing have begun to map her forehead, the area beneath her eyes and her cheekbones. A small circle, almost like a dot but too large to go unnoticed, is tattooed on her left cheek.

'A friend made it with a tattoo machine. It's a reminder of her. Then I was very fair, very healthy. Now I've aged. When you are young, it is a very different thing.'

'A friend? Who was she?' I ask.

'She had this strange name, Chhovi. She was from Bengal. She returned to her village. I never heard from her after that. It's been some fifteen years.'

4

'But Sushma, could she be just any friend? You see the mark she left you every morning in the mirror. She must have been special.'

'We were then living in *teen sau unchaas* number (349). She came there first. Her son, Raju, was five. She was . . . nice. She never squabbled like other women, never spoke ill of other people. She was always cheerful.'

'She was a close friend. Was there anything—anything special— that she did for you, which still means a lot to you? Some favour, some help that you remember?'

'Nothing like that. We shared the same room. We cooked together. When I was ill, she would take me to the doctor. I would do the same for her. I think we both became such good friends because we were so similar. I never fight with anyone either.'

'Do you have a photograph of her?'

'No, there is nothing left of her except in my head. Soofi, I tell you, it is so strange to think of old times.'

'What did Chhovi look like?'

'She was not very beautiful. She was tall . . . now let me see . . . big eyes, black eyes . . . long hair, hmm . . . Bengali women always have long hair. She had a round face. She was fair but not *very* fair. She usually wore salwar suits. She made good fish . . . with gravy . . . her potato sabzi was also good.

'She came from Kolkata. Poor woman. She was from a very poor family. Her husband had left her. I think he was not a good man. But she did not tell me much and I didn't ask. Maybe he was a good man . . . who knows? Anyway, what usually happens to a poor man's wife? Either the man drinks too much, or beats his woman, or both. What can the woman do? Get beaten all her life? You have to give food to your children, right? Somebody from Chhovi's village must have got her here.'

'And she came willingly? Did she know where he was taking her? Did he deceive her?'

'There are people who deceive women into this *dhandha*, this business. But many come willingly. The man must have told her, "Look, this is what you will have to do. If it's not a problem, then you come with me . . ."'

'But Sushma, you know, there's a red light area in Kolkata too. Chhovi could have gone to the Sonagachi red light district there. Why come so far to Delhi?'

'The right thing is to do the dhandha far from home. If you are operating in the same city where you have grown up and where your family lives, then sooner or later your neighbours will find out. People will object. They will say bad things about you. You won't be able to walk with your head up. No one will give you respect.'

'But this man who brought Chhovi to GB Road——I mean, how did he ask her if she wanted to enter the dhandha? You can't propose that to a woman just like that, right?'

'But if a woman tells a man that she is ready to do anything, anything, to make a living, then it becomes clear, in a way, you know. Sometimes you are helpless and you have no choice.'

'And this life in GB Road was better for Chhovi?'

'Her husband had left her. She did not have to worry about him. She earned her own money. Saved some of it. And then she returned home. Today her son must be a grown-up man. He must be earning for her. She must have built her own house, left this line and started her own business, perhaps.'

'Is it possible that she's still doing the dhandha in Kolkata?'

'No one will do this trade in the region where their home is.'

'Did Chhovi have anyone else apart from her husband and son?'

'She had a mother, no father . . . and brothers and sisters. The family, as I told you, was very poor. They didn't know what she was doing here. On visits home, she said she had a job . . . '

'What job?'

'Anything . . . in a hospital or a school. She might have said that she was a servant in a bungalow, washing dishes. But what I feel even now . . . you see, Chhovi and I lived together for seven years. I was in Meerut for a few days when she left. When I returned, I just thought she had gone to meet her folks and that she would be back within a few weeks. She had done that earlier. But fifteen years have passed.'

'And there has been no word from her?'

'No, not even one letter . . . And in those times there were no mobile phones. It hurts when you make friends and they go away. When two people live together and then they separate . . . but *yahan ki dosti, yahin pe khatam*. A friendship that starts in this place always ends in this place. That is a fact.'

'But you still remember Chhovi.'

'Wherever she is right now, she must also be thinking of me sometimes. Of that I'm sure.'

I'M SITTING ON THE KOTHA BALCONY, soaking in the winter sun with Sabir Bhai. How can I describe him? Sabir Bhai is not the owner of the building—that person is somebody else, someone who does not live in GB Road. He is the master of the house, the kotha malik. He rules the kotha. He decides on the woman who stays, and on the ones who are expelled. When the customer gives Rs 120 to Sushma, more than half goes to Sabir Bhai. Sushma calls him 'brother'. I ask him about Sushma. What kind of person is she?

'I don't know,' he says.

'But she has been living in your kotha for five years.'

'Soofi Bhai, a kotha is like a zoo. Today the bird is sitting on this branch. Tomorrow it will fly to another branch. You cannot trust the women here. They keep moving from one kotha to another.'

I lean out to look at GB Road. Traffic is sluggish. The lane going towards Ajmeri Gate is thick with autos, bullock carts, rickshaws, cars, and pull-carts drawn by thin labourers in dhotis. The lane going in the opposite direction is freer, with rickshaws moving smoothly down its course. Occasionally, passengers crane their heads upwards with curiosity. In many kothas, women stand on the balconies and gesture to the men on the road.

Although I'm a blogger who writes on Delhi and its people, I initially started coming to teen sau number as an English teacher. A friend acquainted with Sabir Bhai had told me that a kotha owner in GB Road wanted a tutor for his children. Curious about their world, I had agreed to teach them for free. It was the month of Ramzan. I started with helping the children to introduce themselves in English; the later lessons included colours and describing their favourite movie stars. Over the next few months, they lost interest in English, and the teaching hours dwindled but I still found myself coming to the kotha, fascinated by the ordinary aspects of the lives of people who, I think, have been shepherded by circumstances into living extraordinary lives. It was in an attempt to seek signs of normalcy in an 'abnormal' world that I started to work on this book.

'The same set of women cannot live together in the same kotha for long,' says Sabir Bhai. 'Usually they end up fighting over their livelihood. After all, they are competing for the same customers. In such cases, one of them leaves for another kotha. Some women, I ask them to leave. If they are discourteous to customers or drink too much, for example. Sometimes, I rent out space to a woman who seems decent but who, on getting a rich client downstairs, will take him to some other kotha, where she knows that the kotha malik won't mind if she assaults and robs that client, as long as he gets his share of the loot. This is the most dangerous sort of woman, for she might get you mixed up in a police case.'

'Sushma sounds like a nice woman though.'

'Come on, Soofi Bhai, you can't trust anybody in GB Road. Not even your own woman. I have no faith in Sushma. As long as she is getting along here, it is fine. The truth is that in this line, a husband never trusts his wife, and a wife never trusts her husband. This is the custom. They live together, but they are wary of each other.'

I look at Phalak Begum who is sitting on the floor, by the door, feeding her two-year-old baby. Is she listening to us? Does she agree with Sabir Bhai? What I have made out from my frequent visits to teen sau number is that she is his 'woman'. I'm not sure if they are legally married but they behave like husband and wife. Phalak's four children, all boys, call her Ammi and Sabir Bhai, Abba. Her youngest, though, doesn't look at all like her or Sabir Bhai. While both of them are dark—Sabir Bhai is almost black— the baby, Imran, is almost white. He has blonde hair. As I talk to Sabir Bhai, Imran is sucking on his mother's breast, which Phalak doesn't try to hide under the cover of her dupatta. Is Sabir Bhai wary of her? Has Phalak no faith in him? Does the rule apply to them?

'Yes, Sushma has been living with us for five years but do I know where she is from or who her man is, if she has a man. I know nothing about her. She has not even shared her address. If you ask her, she'll tell you a lie. All the women in GB Road are like that. They never tell you where their home is. They never give any address or phone number. They think that disclosing the address would be risky. Somebody could get in touch with their families who usually don't know about the exact nature of their job. But, you know, when there is a raid and the police arrest them, the women spill everything out. So, you see, they will tell everything about themselves to the police, who in a way are their enemy, but not to the people with whom they live.'

If this is true, then whatever Sushma has told me so far could be just fiction. Her real name may not be Shireen. She may be from somewhere other than Bangalore. She, who speaks Hindi so well, is she actually a north Indian?

I'M WALKING UP TO SUSHMA'S PLACE on the roof of the kotha. The stairs are steep—a common thing in GB Road's kothas—and unlit. On the first landing, I pass a gallery lined with a dozen cell-like rooms. Their doors are closed. There is a washbasin on the right of the gallery. Cardboard boxes of lubricated condoms are piled up in a ventilator's niche. Another flight of stairs, and I'm on the roof. To suddenly step into its openness is startling. The day's blinding light shocks the eye grown used to the darkness of the kotha. It is as if I were on a hilltop. After the heavy mustiness of the kotha, the air here feels thinner.

The front of the roof looks down to GB Road. Across it, the shunting yard of the Indian Railways, and beyond, the budget hotels of Paharganj, a backpackers' district with budget hostels, multi-cuisine cafes, curio shops and second-hand bookstores. On the left is the skyline of Connaught Place. From that blur of high-rises, I can distinguish Parikrama, the revolving restaurant at the top of Antriksh Bhawan, on Kasturba Gandhi Marg, and behind that the muddy-brown Lalit Hotel, as well as the distinctive new headquarters of the Municipal Corporation of Delhi, the twenty-eight-storeyed Dr Shyama Prasad Mukherjee Civic Centre. Looking down from the balustrade, people on the road seem tiny. The noise coming up from the road—the blaring of horns, the tinkling bells of rickshaws and the cries of the vendors—is reduced to a soft hum.

Sushma is not here. I enter her room, a small area covered by a tin roof, without walls. I sit down on a wooden cot. Half of it is taken up by a floppy mattress lying messily in folds. Once, it must have had stripes of colour, now they are faded. The mattress is stained with bird droppings and portions of it have yellowed with layers of dust. A dark blue woollen dhurrie lies folded. On the adjacent cot is a bundle of cotton mats packed in a clean yellow bed-sheet. Beside it is a plastic mug containing a toothbrush, Close-Up toothpaste, a hairbrush and a plastic soap case.

The shed has a jute rope stretched across its length. A threadbare black petticoat is hanging on it, along with a blue salwar kurta and a white bra. Below the cot I'm sitting on are two plastic jars, one is half-filled with rice and the other with salt. There are other things on the floor: a stove, three aluminium bowls, a pressure cooker and a stack of plastic plates. A plastic basket filled with tomatoes, onions, green chillies and garlic sprigs is hanging from the roof of the shed. Beyond the tin shed, there is a stone grinder, used for mashing onions and making chutneys, against the wall. Two buckets lie upside down beside a washbasin built at the back of the kotha's roof. The wall there blocks the view of the Jama Masjid, which is just a dozen roofs away. There is a clay water-pitcher on the balustrade. Crows and pigeons come down, take a dip and fly away. Flower pots are arranged across the length of the roof. Half are planted with chameli flowers; the rest are blooming blue buds of *sadabahar*. Two of these pots are broken. Sushma enters.

'It's getting cold now,' she says. 'Will you have food?'

'Depends on what you are cooking.'

'I'll cook whatever you want. Egg curry?'

'No. But what oil do you use for cooking?'

'Mustard oil. I'm used to mustard oil. At home, we cooked food in refined. But you don't get pure refined here.'

'By home, do you mean Bangalore?'

'Since the time I've left Bangalore, I've been using mustard oil.'

Doubting if Bangalore really was her home, I say, 'Sushma, I've never been to Bangalore. How is it? As hot as Delhi in summer?'

'It's very beautiful. There you get flowers you won't find anywhere else in India. The gardens are like heaven. There are many trees . . .'

'Delhi too has gardens and trees. Have you even been to Lodhi Garden?'

'One garden there . . . cannot remember its name but it has a giant clock, decorated with flowers. And that clock . . . the hands move. The clock tells time. Will you—what should I make?'

'You have *arhar* dal?'

'I can make that. I also have last night's *baingan bhaji*.'

'I want the dal, just boiled . . . '

'Then it'll be bland, it will have no taste. At least let me fry some onions and green chillies.'

'I like the taste of arhar on its own. You can add the fried stuff to your portion.'

'I'll cook some rice.'

'Of course . . . Sushma, I want to ask you something.'

'You'll need a spoon?'

'Yes. Sushma, tell me . . . how did you enter the dhandha?'

'Leave it, Soofi. Why talk of the past? You will have to get the spoon from Bhayya's kitchen downstairs.'

'Tell me, please. I want to know.'

'I had no choice. After Mummy died, the atmosphere at home was not good. Papa wasn't good. He married a new woman. You know what stepmothers are like. She would incite Papa to scold me and my brothers. Every day there would be beatings. She hated us.

'We had an aunt who was living with us. She took good care of us after our mother died. Our stepmother started fighting with her too. Papa was always angry with us. He would side with her. Our stepmother's lie was always the truth, but whatever we had to say was always considered a lie, always.'

'Why are you not putting the lid on the cooker? Just two whistles and the dal will be ready. Won't take more than ten minutes.'

'I cook this way. See the froth rising? Now I'll remove it.'

'Your stepmother was not a good woman—still, what did it have to do with you joining the dhandha?'

'Why talk about her . . . no point . . .'

'I want to know.'

'Well, there was a man living nearby . . . he told me that there was a job in Delhi . . . he was a family friend. He could see I was unhappy. I thought that the job would be something to do with washing clothes or being a servant . . . and I wanted to get away from my stepmother, so one day I left the house and went with him to Delhi.

'You didn't tell your father?'

'No. I still can't believe you want the dal just boiled.'

'Of course, add some salt. And maybe you can chop one tomato for me.'

'Raw? You don't want me to fry it?'

'No, just like this . . . when you reached Delhi, where did you go first?'

'GB Road . . . here . . . I don't remember the kotha number.'

'Did you realize the kind of place it was?'

'Not for the first two days . . . but then . . . I don't know . . . and then they forced me into this.

'It dawned gradually that this was a red light area. First I was just confused. Then I grew doubtful when the kotha malik started telling me that I would have to do this kind of work.

'I was told I would have to talk to men, and I would have to do all that, you know, which a woman does with a man after marriage.'

Sushma laughs.

'I initially refused, but then I had no choice.'

'Why are you saying that?'

'I had come too far. I could not return home. I worked in that kotha for a few months and then I became free. I started operating on my own.'

15

'Which means that when you were working independently, you could choose to refuse a man if you didn't like him?'

'There is no question of like and dislike in this line. The customer just needs to have the money to pay. You don't care whether he is fat or black or old. I actually thought that I would earn a good amount of money and then return home and live with my brothers in a separate house.'

'Did you return?'

'. . . Papa refused to see me.'

'Did you tell him what you had started doing?'

'No. But these things are difficult to hide. You know how things are. If a girl leaves her home even for a night, all honour is lost. See, the dal is ready.'

'But Sushma . . .'

'Leave it, Soofi. Enough. I don't want to remember old things.'

'Are you crying?'

'Don't be silly. It's the onions . . . now this is life. It started somewhere else but here in GB Road it will end.'

'Sushma, the sun looks so beautiful.'

'Yes. In the mountains, when the sun sets, it feels very nice. But I'm so hungry. I haven't eaten since I woke up in the afternoon. Just brushed my teeth and nothing else. Will you go down to get the spoon?'

'THE DAL IS VERY GOOD, SUSHMA.'

'Really? But you must have some *baghaar*. I'm frying onions and chillies for myself.'

'No, go on, but give me some green chillies. Sushma, do you have any children?'

She shakes her head.

'I'm sure you must have loved someone, some man.'

16

'Hmm . . . yes, there was one. I spent twenty years with him, more than the years I spent with my parents.

'Prem. His full name was Prem Kumar. He used to paint cars. He had a garage in Karol Bagh. He loved me so much.'

A long pause while I eat and Sushma fries onions for her dal.

'Never ever did that man ask me what I had to offer him. He would always give, give and give. He never made me suffer from any want. He gave me money regularly. In those years, I always cooked in ghee, not mustard oil. He liked my dry meat and aloo palak.'

'How did you meet him?'

'He came as a customer, and started visiting me often. One day he came and then never went back.'

'He had a family?'

'Yes. A wife, a son, a daughter-in-law . . . he would meet them once a week.'

'Did they object to you?'

'No, they were nice people. Sometimes he would take me to meet them. They told me that if he was happier with me, then he could live with me.'

'So, then what happened?'

'I moved to Meerut and he followed me there. One day he was on the roof; it had no railing and he fell. I took him to the hospital but he died within a week. He was a Hindu, so we cremated him.'

'You did not inform his family?'

'Much later. They asked me why I had not told them earlier but they understood.'

'Who cremated him?'

'A son of my friend. He was very close to that child. I arranged the cremation, the boy lit the pyre.'

It is evening. I'm at a friend's place in Nizamuddin East. I'm tired but there is a long night ahead.

17

'So, what are you doing tonight?' she asks, as we eat dinner. She has cooked pasta in white sauce. There is wine.

'I'll be going to GB Road.'

'GB Road! Why?'

'I'll spend the night there.'

'Ah, good for you.'

Perhaps she thinks I am going there for sex.

I want to be with Sushma when she goes down to the corridor at three in the morning to solicit customers. Once she gets a man, she takes him upstairs to the cell Sabir Bhai has allotted to her for work. Later, she comes down again to wait for more men. I want to see how Sushma conducts herself on the street. How does she look after putting on her make-up? How easily does she get customers? How many men does she get in those four hours? How long does each appointment last? What does she do while waiting for men to come to her? What does she talk about during the wait? I want to know all these things.

IT IS ABOUT 11 O'CLOCK and Sushma is sleeping. I want to go up to her place on the roof and see how anyone can sleep there on such a cold night. I ask ten-year-old Osman to accompany me. He is the second of Sabir Bhai's four sons: Omar is twelve, Masoom, eight, and then there is the two-year-old Imran. Osman is scared of the dark. Phalak, his mother, tells him to be a man. He steels himself and I follow him. On the roof, we can see the late-night traffic on the railway bridge that spans the New Delhi station. The neon lights on the hotels of Paharganj blink at regular intervals. My eyes rest on the giant electric billboard of Hotel Mohun International—Government Approved. The high-rises of Connaught Place are cloaked in darkness. So is our roof. The blanket on Sushma's bed is rumpled as if there is a cat inside it. That can't be her. So where is she?

'She's probably sleeping inside the box room,' says Osman.

While going down he shows me the alcove, a small landing sandwiched between two floors. The door is closed. Two plastic slippers are placed outside. If Sushma wakes up in the middle of night, can she sit without her head hitting the roof?

AFTER SETTING MY ALARM for 3, I lie down to read a short-story collection. My bed has been made in what used to be a storeroom on one side of the entrance hall—something like a cupboard, really. The women have laid down their mattresses on the floor in the hall and in a room that opens on to the kotha's balcony. Sabir Bhai, who has a separate room with a TV and a single cot, is chatting with me. This is the first time I am staying the night in GB Road and I am a little nervous.

'Are the doors open throughout the night?' I ask Sabir Bhai.

'Sushma and Fatima have to work at night so we close them only in the morning,' he says.

'Oh, Fatima too? Doesn't she make chai for Sushma in the morning?'

'Yes, but she has already made it. It's in the thermos.'

'But Sabir Bhai, isn't it scary? The door remains open. Anybody can come in . . . what about criminals?'

'Soofi Bhai, this is the risk we have to take. We have no choice. Sometimes bad characters do come. That is why, in case of any trouble, I stay awake all night long. I go to sleep at eight in the morning. You know, I've had bad experiences in the past. Sometimes you get a customer who shouts bad words, brandishes a knife or a pistol, or smashes a beer bottle against the wall. Once a drunkard tried to hit me on the head. But we cannot close the door.'

As I draw a thick quilt over me, Osman tells me the plot of *Dabangg*, the film that stars his favourite actor, Salman Khan. I ask him about Sushma instead. 'She is different from other women,' he says. 'She cooks good food, is nice to people, never fights and wears clean clothes.'

It is 5.30 in the morning. I haven't heard the alarm. Everyone is sleeping but I can see there is a light in Sabir Bhai's room. I get out of bed and silently walk down the stairs.

'Soofi,' Sushma greets me, in a cheery long-time-no-see kind of tone. She is sitting down on a large stone, on which she has placed a shawl wrapped in a polythene bag. Fatima has a similarly cushioned seat. They have placed themselves on either side of the door. It is freezing. For the first time I see GB Road bare of traffic. The corridor is empty, save for a few groups of women huddled together in front of different kothas. At irregular intervals, the long boom of rail engines pierces the silence.

Towards the pillars, where the corridor gives way to a drain that skirts the road, orange sparks die out in freshly burnt wood. 'I lit the fire at 4,' Sushma says.

'This is not cold. Wait for December and it will be so foggy that you won't be able to see anything on the road,' says Fatima.

'Even then you sit here from 3 to 7?'

'Yes,' says Sushma. 'I don't know what I'll do. I haven't got even one customer.'

'The bloody police were scaring off the clients,' says Fatima.

'Bloody motherfuckers! They don't say anything when other women call out to clients during the day. But when it was my time, they sat up here like bastards,' says Sushma, who utters the swear words so casually that they don't sound like expletives. She is wearing a pale-pink salwar suit with a cream shawl. She has put on brown lipstick. Since it is dark, I can't see her face clearly, but she does not look like the cliché of an over-made-up prostitute. She could pass for a mother of teenagers getting ready for an evening outing to India Gate.

As a man approaches, I go and sit by the dying fire, warming my hands. He is carrying a bag on his shoulders. Sushma rushes to him, saying, '*Aa, aa, aaja.*' He keeps walking. 'Come on man, stop, stop for just a minute. Look, just stop man.' The man keeps walking.

Had the man agreed to go upstairs with Sushma, I wonder, after how many minutes would they have returned? And how quickly would Sushma have got ready again? Would she have cleaned herself? Does she take a bath each time she entertains a client? Does she use condoms? I'm curious but I cannot ask her these questions. I would be uncomfortable if someone got curious about my sex life.

But why is Fatima here? She is frail and old. Her hair is grey and her eyes are sunken. She hasn't even put on any make-up. How can she get a customer? Why would any man come to her? What goes on in her mind when young men sleep with her?

'Soofi, you are shivering,' Fatima says. 'Go, go up. There is still time for some more sleep.'

'No, I'm fine,' I say. 'If there was a lamp here, I could have brought my book from upstairs.'

We see a young man is coming. Sushma goes out into the road. 'Hey, where are you going? Come, just listen, man. Hey.' The man looks at her. 'Shh, come.'

Another man appears. Fatima says, '*Aa, aa, sun toh.* Listen.' Neither of them stops.

I'm worried. Sushma must get a customer.

'When I was putting on make-up, I was feeling sweaty,' says Sushma. 'I knew it would be colder.'

'What is the connection?' I ask.

'When it is warm and suffocating inside a closed room, it means that it is very windy outside,' Sushma says.

An autorickshaw is coming down from Ajmeri Gate. Sushma shouts, '*Oye* auto. Auto will bring my man. Come.' The auto keeps going and soon we lose sight of it.

'Soofi,' Fatima says. 'Why don't you cut your hair?'

'Yes, Soofi,' says Sushma. 'It's looking very ba—hey, another man! But no, he is looking weighed down with debts.'

We laugh.

'Soofi, are you a Sikh?' Fatima asks.

'It is the last day of the month,' says Sushma. 'People will get their wages by the second or the third . . . '

'Then they will have money to spend here,' says Fatima.

'By the fifteenth all their money will be gone,' says Sushma.

'Hey, look,' I exclaim, spotting three young men in jackets and jeans.

'*Na re*, they won't come. They have spent the night here and are now going home,' Sushma says.

'How do you know?' I ask.

'Didn't you hear them talking about money?' Sushma says. 'Who spent how much on what.'

The first light of morning begins to show. A boy in a red jacket is sweeping the corridor, raising clouds of dust. Sushma walks down the walkway and turns left into a lane. After ten minutes she returns carrying pieces of discarded wooden furniture.

'Got it in front of Barkat's tea stall. He is making the tea. Call Sumaira. She will bring three glasses for us.' Sumaira, another woman in the kotha, has been so ill for the past few years that she is no longer able to sleep with customers. To make herself useful, she does menial jobs for everyone else, like getting bidis, beer, milk, vegetables or chai.

As the day gets brighter, I notice a puppy sleeping by the side of the staircase.

'He is a bastard,' Sushma says, laughing.

'There are many dogs on this road and when a motorcycle or a car passes, they run after it as if they would eat the car as well as the driver,' Fatima says.

23

'Once a man was riding a bike when they went after him,' Sushma says. 'And he got so scared that he fell off.'

'Do these dogs bite?' I ask.

'No,' Sushma says. 'I know all of them.' And suddenly after saying this, she gets up and starts calling out, '*Ai, aa, aaja, oye aa.*' And the dogs start coming, from behind the pillars, rubbish bins and closed paan stalls. They gather around, sniffing me as if I'm fresh meat.

'No, don't worry,' Sushma says, lovingly shooing off the dogs. 'They are bastards but nice. They are just testing you. You are a new face.'

As I hesitantly pat a brown dog, afraid of its tongue-flapping friendliness, Sumaira arrives with the chai. 'How are you?' I ask. We are sitting by the fire.

'I'm fine but my chest hurts.'

A few days ago Sabir Bhai had showed me an X-ray of Sumaira's. The doctor said one of her kidneys has disintegrated. As Sumaira sat blank-eyed by my side, Sabir Bhai said she did not have long to live. While sipping the milky tea, I want to hold her hands. But I cannot bring myself to touch her. Her face looks greasy, her clothes are unwashed, her nails are dark green with dirt and she smells as if she hadn't taken a bath for days.

Suddenly, I feel revolted. By Sumaira, by the sickly sweet milky chai, by all the people in GB Road.

'I must leave now,' I declare, standing up. 'I'll come tonight, Sushma.'

'Why?' she asks.

'I want to spend the entire shift, from 3 in the morning, with you. I woke up so late today.'

'No, Soofi, you mustn't sit out here,' Sushma says. 'It is not a good place. The police come often. It is not the place for you.'

'I'll come.'

I'M DRINKING RED WINE. One of my friends, a French designer friend is going home for good. A farewell party has been organized for her in an apartment in Sujan Singh Park. I don't know anyone here except the said French friend, so I'm sitting by myself on one of the sofas, sipping a wine whose name I cannot pronounce. The guests look like confident and successful people. There is a former cabinet minister, two senior journalists, a fashion designer, an ayurveda entrepreneur, a hotelier, a painter. An art gallery director is slouching on the other sofa. The fiancée of a young politician is standing beside her mother, a culture tsarina of her time. A crowd has gathered around a professor of erotica, who is expounding on symbols in eighth-century Indian art. A white woman is warming her hands by the fireside.

I have promised Sushma I would sit with her tonight. But the wine makes me drowsy. The people here are well-dressed and clean. Uniformed servants are laying out the dinner. Silver cutlery has been placed on the table.

I'll go to GB Road tomorrow.

I COME OUT ON TO THE ROOF. Sushma is standing against the balustrade. She is in a light-blue salwar suit with a shawl wrapped around her. The sun has set, leaving behind streaks of orange and pink in the sky. Sushma does not know I'm here. She is talking on a mobile phone. Something is cooking on the stove. I sit down on the bed. I have a bag that I discreetly keep under the bed. A few minutes pass.

Who is she talking to? I can hear her saying '*bhabhi*', a term to address a brother's wife. Sushma had told me that she was not in touch with her family. Then who is this bhabhi? I think of Sabir Bhai's words. Can I trust this woman? Of the stories she has told me, how many are true?

'Soofi, it is you,' Sushma turns around. 'When did you arrive? I'm making *bathua* saag. Stay and have some.' She tucks the cellphone in her cleavage.

'Who was on the phone?'

'A friend.'

'You call her bhabhi?'

'Yes. She lives in Meerut. She is my landlord's wife. We are good friends. After coming to Delhi, I stayed in GB Road for two or three years. There are many women here who have also worked in Meerut. The red light area there is in Kabadi Bazaar. I lived there for many years.'

'So this landlady too is in this dhandha?'

'No, they live in Gudri Bazaar. All my belongings are there. Bed, table, clothes, lamps . . .'

'Will you take me there some day?'

'No. I can't take men there. They gave me the room on that condition. Besides, Gudri Bazaar is a dangerous area. I will never let you go there. It is full of Muslims.'

'You are saying this as if you weren't one!'

'People there are quick to get into fights. Very dangerous place. But I like that room. It has been mine for twelve years. Bhabhi and her children have grown close to me.'

'So, Prem lived with you in that room?'

'No, I was in Kabadi Bazaar at that time. You are having saag with me?'

'I see you have already added mustard oil . . .'

'Soofi, look at you. Your hair is greying. You must marry before it is too late.'

'You never married.'

'Why marry in this line of work?'

The strains of a bhajan drift from some nearby temple.

'You should marry. Then you will have children and they will earn for you when you are old. I had one, but he died within a month. I used to call him Bablu. He would have been fifteen.'

'Who was his father?'

'Who knows?'

'Maybe Prem?'

'Maybe. Maybe not.'

A railway engine gives a long whistle.

'Soofi, come at noon some day and I will put mehndi and chai *patti* paste on your hair. It will bring some shine.'

I go to the balustrade and look for the temple. The bhajan's echoing hum is spreading, drowning out all the sounds of the evening, including that of the traffic, but the gathering darkness has reduced the buildings to their edges, and the temple is difficult to spot. Its bells start ringing. The muezzin of the nearby mosque starts calling for the *maghrib*, or evening, prayers. *Allah hu Akbar*. Sushma is washing rice. Suddenly remembering, I turn towards the bed, pick up my bag and take out a white cashmere shawl. It belonged to my mother. I walk behind Sushma and wrap it around her shoulders. She gently pats my hand.

No rooms of
their own

GB Road is a stone's throw from the New Delhi Railway
Station. If you take the station's Ajmeri Gate exit, it is a mere
ten-minute walk.

From Green Park metro station, the closest stop to my home
in the fashionable Hauz Khas Village, it is a twenty-minute ride.
Outside peak hours, it is possible to find an empty seat, press my
nose against the book of the day and read in peace until the train
pulls into New Delhi railway station.

Outside the metro station, there is nothing to tell you that
the sex workers' quarters are so close. There are two coffee kiosks
near the station entrance, a food court, and a tree with two trunks,
one of them bending towards the roof of the coffee kiosk, as if
it wants a swig, too, and the other spreading out a sunshade of
leafy branches. A peepul tree outside the food court shelters a
cigarette vendor.

The Kamla Market clock tower stands across the road, its arms
forever frozen at 11.15.

I take a left turn and GB Road is still out of sight. The smell
of the street announces that it doubles as a public loo. There is
urine almost everywhere; it fills a shallow ditch along the side of
the road and pockmarks the pavement in puddles. This seems
to be a feast for the flies. A number of them buzz over the filth.

People step into the puddles and, walking onwards, leave their footprints on the drier parts.

Ahead are two gutters. Dark grey waste, taken out of these sewers, has been left on the pavement. Two thin men sit by these mounds of muck, deep in conversation. The stench refuses to leave me, as if it was stuck to my shirt.

The next hurdle on the way to GB Road is the toughest: the square. There are traffic lights at five places but not a single one works. Cops in white shirts and navy blue trousers stand at the corner, at the entrance to Kamla Market, pretending not to notice the chaos. Buses, bullock carts, Matadors, mini-trucks, rickshaws, pull-carts, scooters, bikes, buses and pedestrians make their way through this everyman's land like a ragtag band of vagabonds walking down a dirt track. Entering the fray, I run a few steps, slow down to skirt a tractor, stop for a bus to pass, bypass a bullock cart, and finally attach myself to another pedestrian, tailing him closely as he confidently dodges the vehicles.

On the other side, I keep to the left of the pavement. Dope addicts lie on the ground, right outside the fortification of the Anglo-Arabic School. A student jumps out of one of the niches in the boundary wall. Outside the school gate is a police post, where a display banner exhorts the passers-by to 'Be our eyes and ears'.

Enterprise thrives here. A part of the pavement is taken over by a tailor who pedals his sewing machine under a neem tree. Next to him is a man with a telephone booth, which consists of three Tata Indicom phones arranged on a wooden table. Next is a barber squatting on the floor, trimming the moustache of a customer. Then, GB Road.

THE AREA'S PRINCIPAL LANDMARK lies just before the entrance to GB Road. Ajmeri Gate is a seventeenth-century gateway. In

Mughal times, this sturdy signpost was the exit point for royal processions on their way to Ajmer, the Sufi pilgrim town west of Delhi. Every day, thousands of migrants step out of the New Delhi Railway Station and the first significant landmark they see—or rather see through—is Ajmeri Gate. As do the daily-wage labourers walking past the ruin, dragging heavy loads with their bare arms. Beggars take a siesta on its border wall. Autos and cycle rickshaws are parked at its entrance. Hundreds of women from villages across the country come every year to live in the gateway's immediate vicinity to work as prostitutes.

When a prospective sex worker first reaches Delhi by train and heads to GB Road, she is likely to emerge from the railway station, not the metro stop. The woman might be alone or not. She might be entering the trade voluntarily or it could be a 'friend' duping her into it.

On getting off the train and emerging from the station, what are her first impressions of Delhi? What buildings does she see? What sounds does she hear? What idea does she get of the city where she will spend a significant part of her life, a city whose men will pay to have sex with her?

Standing on the station's footbridge that spans the platforms and rail tracks, I try looking for GB Road landmarks: the kothas on the first and second floors. It is late evening and the neon signs are obstructing the view. Far away, in the other direction, looms a tower. Some of its floors are lit up, while others are dark. A giant crane is slowly moving its jib by its side. A new building is coming up in the area.

GB Road is a red light district, but it is other things too. It most noticeably hosts a wholesale market of sanitaryware—washbasins, bath tubs, dressing mirrors and water closets are usually seen taking over the arcades, which at night shelter the homeless labourers. There are other shops too, selling water pumps, generators and steel bearings. Banks, ATMs, a temple, a mosque and a police post also dot the area. There are many trees too.

Yet, the borders are clearly demarcated. If sanitaryware showrooms and other businesses flourish on the ground floor, kothas stick to the upper floors. Outside teen sau number, where Sushma, Sabir Bhai and others live, there are no trees.

THERE ARE EIGHTY KOTHAS in GB Road's forty-two buildings. Each has its owner (called a malik), women and, occasionally, pimps. The kothas are reached through ill-lit stairs built in gaps between the shops on the covered walkway. There are twenty-one sets of stairs. Each kotha is twenty feet wide and twelve feet high. The length is about forty feet. The kothas share a similar design, save a few alterations depending on the whims of the malik. There is always a large sitting room, the first place that a customer enters. Wooden benches are arranged along the wall for the women to sit on. One side of the hall opens to a room used for singing and dancing, a tradition that is dying. The other side leads to a small private room for the kotha malik. All her personal belongings—luggage, saris, gods, TV, cash box—are kept there. The room is deliberately built next to the sitting room so that the malik can keep an eye on the kind of people coming into the kotha.

The kitchen is in the back area. So is the bathroom. The balcony—the only open place in the kotha—is at the front, facing the road. Many kothas have women standing there to attract customers. The gallery between the dancing room and the balcony is lined with cell-like chambers with shuttered doors. Here the women 'entertain' the clients.

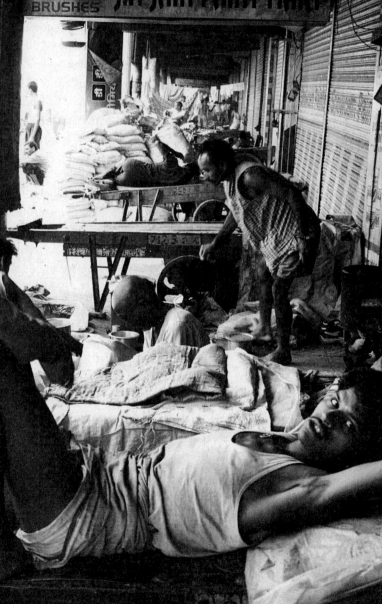

The women have no rooms of their own. At night, the singing room is converted into a dormitory. The floor is swept clean, mattresses are laid out, and the women go to sleep, unless they are at work. Every woman, of course, has her personal possessions, such as money, saris, jewellery, make-up kit, family photo albums and glossy film magazines. Most of them are packed into their own luggage, which is stored in an attic—called the *tehkhana*—built into the false roof. These attics are spacious and one can comfortably sit in them. The tehkhana has other purposes, too. When a woman's betrayed lover angrily storms into the kotha with a knife or a pistol hunting for her, she usually hides in this attic. When there is a police raid and a woman doesn't want to be caught, she climbs up into the attic and waits there till the police leave.

Sometimes, when a woman has been forcibly brought into a kotha, or she is a minor, and the police are making their rounds, the malik forces her to hide in the tehkhana and threatens her against crying out to alert the cops. In 2001, the *Times of India* carried a story on underage girls rescued from one such tehkhana:

10 minor girls rescued from GB Road

On its second raid conducted within a month, Delhi Police has rescued ten minor girls from the red light area of GB Road in central Delhi, police said on Friday. On the basis of information provided by one of the 38 girls rescued on August 17, [a] raid was conducted by [the] police on a kotha and [they] released the minor girls kept in a tehkhana (secret room), police said. Two managers of the brothel, Saira and Manjula, have been arrested along with six pimps, police said, adding a search was on to nab the brothel owner and the lady who had brought the girls to the place.

TEEN SAU NUMBER IS HOME TO FIVE WOMEN—Sushma, Nighat, Phalak, Fatima and Sumaira. Phalak, a mother of four boys, says she has ceased to be a sex worker but I could not be sure. Sumaira, whose kidney has been destroyed completely, doesn't work because she complains of excruciating pain while having sex. Sushma and Fatima work in the early morning hours. Nighat is the only woman who works during the day. She never goes down into the corridor to get customers; neither does she lure them by standing in the balcony. She waits for clients in the sitting room instead.

THE CURIOUS THING ABOUT TEEN SAU NUMBER is that its malik is not a woman. I enter Sabir Bhai's room. It has a bed, a coffee-coloured wooden table, a refrigerator and an open drawer stacked with some Hindi books: *Dilli Jo Ek Sheher hai* (Delhi, the City That Is), *Kamasutra*, Kautilya's *Arthshashtra* and *Kanooni Salah, Aapke Liye* (Legal Advice, For You). Kautilya's seventh-century treatise on statecraft is wrapped in cellophane. One wall of the room has a calendar showing Mecca. Another has a giant poster of Lakshmi, Ganesha and Saraswati.

Sabir Bhai is watching the Hindi news on Doordarshan. It is about 3 in the afternoon and Phalak is brushing her teeth and, at the same time, washing the floor. Nighat brings buckets full of water which she pours on to the floor, and Phalak sweeps it clean with a straw broom. Both have their salwars folded up to their knees. Sushma is in the sitting room, a blanket wrapped around her.

Watching the women clean his room, Sabir Bhai says, 'The kothas should not be filthy. Customers should not cringe on entering. The maliks spend money from their own pockets; landlords don't contribute. They live in *samaaj*, society, and they have nothing to do with the dhandha. They get their monthly rent of a fixed amount. The earning goes only to the women and the malik.

'The character of the kotha depends on the malik alone. If he has no moral issues, he would buy women who have been duped into coming to GB Road. He would have contacts with pimps who bring women from their poor, remote villages with promises of respectable employment in big cities. Some maliks even keep minor girls. I never do that. I have to show my face to Allah.'

A man enters the veranda. Nighat rolls down her salwar, leaves the bucket with Phalak and goes up to the new arrival with a big smile on her face, 'So, you've come.' The man seems to be in his sixties. Nighat seems to be in her mid-twenties. She takes him upstairs. Unlike other kothas, the cells in teen sau number are built on the floor above. Though there is one cell—big enough for only a single bed—just behind the veranda, next to the kitchen.

'So, I was saying that earlier the kothas looked nicer,' Sabir Bhai says. 'There were more customers, more business, and so more money to spend on beautifying the buildings. This kotha was built by my landlord's grandfather. The floors were originally laid with half-inch-thick tiles that had flowers painted on them. Over the years, some tiles cracked, some came off, and they were replaced with new tiles, which are plain, thin and dull.'

The floor of Sabir Bhai's room is laid with dark grey square tiles. They give the room the appearance of a bathroom. A bowl of dried grapes lies on a pile of newspapers, beside the TV. Sabir Bhai takes out one, rips it open with his fingers, removes the seed and offers it to me. I hesitate. Sabir Bhai sneezes, without covering his mouth, and insists that I have the grape. For fear of offending him, I take it.

NO ONE LIVES HERE. The door is open. The floor is dusty. Cobwebs hang from the ceiling fan. The glass windows are broken. This is a

kotha one floor below Sabir Bhai's establishment. Facing number 298, it has been lying vacant for a few months. The women living here left after a police raid. Three minor girls were discovered hidden in the tehkhana.

I walk towards the balcony. It is shut off by a *khus* screen. Sunlight streams through the vertical slits in the screen's weave, making a slanting pattern on the floor. The gallery is dark and musty. The cells are closed. I try opening one. The door is jammed. The dancing hall has its roof done up with polished Sunmica set on a plywood panel. Where could the tehkhana be?

Sabir Bhai had told me that the first occupant of this kotha was a woman called Maya Devi. She was a kotha malik, but, he had said, she was also an accomplished Hindustani classical singer, especially trained in thumri and *dadra*. If her admirers insisted, however, she would also sing bhajans. I climb back to Sabir Bhai's kotha.

'Maya Devi died in the 1970s,' Sabir Bhai tells me. 'I never met her. She was from Shimla. With a huge following among Delhi's rich, she was one of the most respected people in the community. Singers and dancers would come from Kolkata and Bombay with their problems. She used to sing ghazals at the Red Fort. She also danced. She had pictures taken with Jawaharlal Nehru. Everyone, including the customers, gave her respect.'

'And then?'

'And then what . . . she died. And then the Emergency came and everything changed.'

In June 1975, the Indira Gandhi government, besieged by the Opposition and the judiciary, declared a state of Emergency in the country, suspending all elections and civil liberties. Politicians were arrested, organizations were banned and thousands of protesters were thrown into jail. During this twenty-one-month period, Sanjay Gandhi, Mrs Gandhi's son and her closest political adviser, decided to get rid of all the supposed ills of India, especially of Delhi, in one stroke. Slums in the Jama Masjid area were demolished. Men in the crowded Turkman Gate neighbourhood were forced to undergo sterilization. GB Road was not spared either. Before the Emergency, the police rarely stepped into a kotha. That exemption ended with the Emergency. The beat constables became as familiar as the pimps.

The Emergency marks the beginning of the decline of GB Road. The singing and dancing became less popular. The city's sophisticates stopped coming. The thumris and dadras gave way to film songs. Some kothas got rid of their sitars and equipped their dancing room with revolving 'disco lights'. Gradually, the dancing and singing, too, lost their point. Customers begin to expect immediate sex. Cells became more important than dancing halls.

Lately, even the cells have started becoming irrelevant. Gone are the days when a city needed to have a separate red light district. Massage parlours, beauty salons and friendship clubs offering sex on the pretext of other services have opened across Delhi. The red light has gone out into the city. GB Road has been left behind.

I'M WALKING DOWN THE CORRIDOR towards Ajmeri Gate. A plump old woman in a red shawl and a crumpled green nightie is calling me. I keep going straight. A pimply boy has started following me. He is whispering into my ears, 'N Joy. N joy. N joy.' I ask him to leave. He is determined. 'Assamese, Nepali, Bengali, Bihari, Punjabi, Gujarati . . . just come upstairs. No money for looking at the girls . . .'

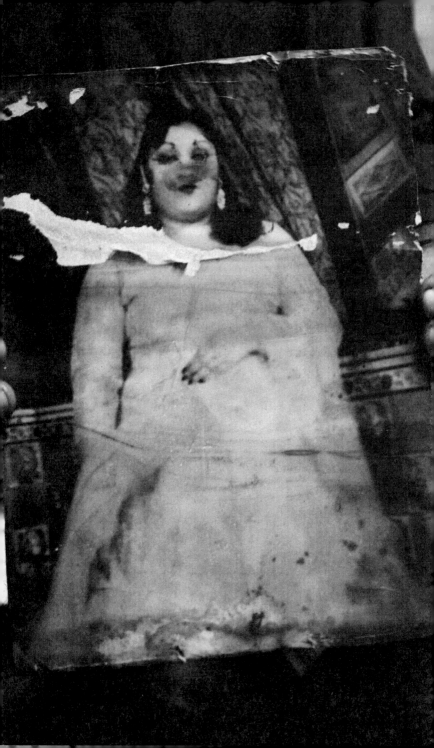

'Not interested. Go away!' I say.

'If you don't like the girls, no problem.'

'Look, don't follow me.'

'You want minor?'

I don't respond.

'Nepalis are very fair.'

He keeps following me and I start walking faster. He's most probably harmless. But Sabir Bhai has warned me against pimps. According to him, they are petty criminals on the run from the police of their hometowns. What if this pimp grabs my arm and doesn't let go? I'm thin and weak. What if he drags me upstairs and pins me down with a knife? If he snatches my wallet . . . What if I'm killed in a fight?

To die in GB Road!

My poor parents.

I HAVE BEGUN TO SPEND a few hours in GB Road almost daily. The pull is mysterious. The area is not scenic. The men are loud and aggressive. The women are pushy and unappealing. The street lingo is full of mother–sister swear words. Drunkards lie on the corridor. Customers gather outside the staircases of the kothas, staring at the women inviting them in.

The area's finer aesthetics are almost impossible to spot and their beauty difficult to cherish. For instance, the corridor has delicately carved pillars, just like the ones in Chandni Chowk, but their prettiness is dampened by the drainage ditch running alongside. Similarly, a few kothas on the left-hand side of the road have windows, balconies and roofs very similar in design to some of Shahjahanabad's most beautiful surviving havelis, but that is because the maliks have never cared to renovate those kothas.

Women such as Nighat have beautiful features but that natural loveliness gets hidden under layers of make-up.

Occasionally, Sabir Bhai insists that I have a meal with him. That is the most difficult part. I don't like their food. There is oil floating on the gravy, the vegetables are overcooked such that they become unrecognizable and I know that the plate on which I would be served the rice was washed below the washbasin area, where Imran, the little blonde one, pees and where the women spit while brushing their teeth. But I cannot refuse the invitation. If I don't eat their food, and drink their unfiltered water, why would the people of GB Road share the stories of their lives with me?

EVERY NOW AND THEN, GB Road gets to me and spending another minute in this depressing world becomes unbearable. Sometimes while chatting with Nighat in the sitting room as she waits for customers, or watching Sushma cook her meal on the rooftop, I try to picture the Delhi that lies beyond GB Road. The Khan Market bookstores, the Mehrauli ruins, the Saket malls, the date cake (with hot toffee sauce) served at Café Turtle . . . and all of it seems unreal.

My life outside of GB Road takes a beating. Does my one-room apartment in Hauz Khas really look out on to the ruins? Do I have friends other than Sabir Bhai or Sushma? Whenever I feel overwhelmed, I rush out of teen sau number, walk down the stairs, race through the corridor, and without looking back at Ajmeri Gate even once, and head to the Delhi I'm comfortable with. I walk past the metro entrance, leave the railway station behind, cross the Minto Bridge underpass, cross the Outer Circle and reach Connaught Place. Only then I relax. I walk to the Inner Circle, dawdle aimlessly, look at shoppers and tourists. Finally, I head to D Block. Once inside the Embassy restaurant, ensconced in a world of hushed conversations and uniformed stewards, I order a club sandwich and Darjeeling tea, grateful to be back to what then appears to me as 'civilization'. I take a novel from my shoulder bag and forget about GB Road.

IT's THE BEGINNING OF DECEMBER and the fog has settled around Ajmeri Gate. With gusts of cold wind sharply slapping my face, I walk, hands in my pockets, wanting to see GB Road as a night-time customer. Few street lamps are lit. Shops are closed. Stoves are glowing red on two omelette carts below the peepul tree. A man is peeing against a closed paan stall. There are rows of parked autos too. A group of boys are bargaining for rates with an auto-wallah. The arcades are completely dark but the golden glow of a street lamp falls on a man sleeping on the ground. He is under a quilt. A dog sleeps by his side, sharing his mattress.

My eyes are slowly getting used to the darkness. A labourer is sleeping on a wooden pull-cart. I see another pull-cart, another labourer. The staircases to the kothas are lit by single electric lamps. Men in jeans and leather jackets. One middle-aged man is dressed formally in trousers, jacket and tie. A white Corolla moves down the road, stopping outside the entrance of each kotha. The men in the car roll down the windows to have a look at the women calling out from the staircases.

I stop outside a kotha and look. Up the stairs, a woman is sitting by a lamp. She is wearing a shiny green salwar and a red cardigan. Her body is bone-thin and her face is covered with dark spots. She signals me to come up. I shake my head, give a nervous smile and walk ahead. The next staircase has four women hidden in the shadows on the first landing. One is wearing only a salwar and a bra. She smiles, showing her paan-stained teeth. A couple of men are gathered at the entrance. I join the crowd. The women are calling out to us in hushed tones.

'*Aaja.*'

'Listen to me.'

'Just one minute. Come up.'

One points her finger at me and says in English, 'Come.'

I turn and start going further down the corridor. Two young pimps start following me. 'Where are you going?' one of them asks.

I start walking faster.

'Chinese for 800.'

I'm trying not to show my anxiety.

'We have Russian, too.'

'You are wasting your time.'

They turn back.

At number 242, half a dozen women stand chatting. They ignore me. A wooden bench lies vacant. Suddenly one woman pushes another on to the bench and climbs over her as if she is a man trying to force herself on her. They laugh. It is a sport. Suddenly, they get up and rush upstairs, saying in a hushed tone, 'Go, go go, gogogo . . . ' A white jeep comes to a stop. Cops step out and the men in the street start running. I run for teen sau number, and go up the stairs. It's completely dark and I stumble into a few women of the left-hand-side kotha, just below Sabir Bhai's establishment. They must have been standing outside and had stepped in as the jeep appeared. They are waiting for the cops to leave. I rush to the second floor and enter teen sau. Nighat is sleeping on a mattress laid out on the floor. Sushma must be upstairs. I go to the other room. Sabir

Bhai, Phalak, Omar, Osman and Masoom are watching *Bigg Boss* on TV. On seeing me, they look surprised for a moment and then delightedly exclaim, 'Soofi!'

I'm home.

There were Persian carpets on the floor

As I walk through Delhi, my fellow traveller is Ronald Vivian Smith's *The Delhi That No-one Knows*. It is a book on the city's myths, legends, rumours and secrets.

In the book's introduction, Smith writes:

> I did not refer to any book, did not make notes from dusty volumes in old libraries—I just walked! Sometimes I took buses—many a long afternoon years ago, when as a bachelor and a young journalist in Delhi, finding out about old monuments was a passion.

One evening, a friend in Nizamuddin East mentioned in passing that many years ago Smith had had a crush on her and that he had written a love poem for her in his newspaper column. She said he was then known in literary circles for initiating people into the art of love-making, guiding them to the best courtesans in town, teaching the correct way of eating paan, explaining how to tie a *gajra*, and how to talk of love to the beloved. He had lovers in GB Road.

I wanted to meet this man.

Of all the authors who have made Delhi a central theme of their literary lives, Smith is among the most intriguing. He has given much to the city, but the city has held back. Author of several slim volumes on Delhi's monuments and street life. Smith has also produced novels and poetry. Yet he has been denied the eminence enjoyed by other Delhi chroniclers.

Born in Agra, Smith graduated in English literature from that city's St. John's College. He came to Delhi in 1961 and became a sub-editor-cum-reporter for the Press Trust of India. Two years later he joined the *Statesman*, from which he retired as news editor in 1997. His columns continue sporadically in *The Hindu* and the *Statesman*.

Before moving to Mayapuri in west Delhi in 1978, Smith lived in the historical districts of Delhi: Civil Lines, Matia Mahal and Daryaganj. 'It was a difficult change from Old Delhi to west Delhi,' he tells me. We are sitting at a window-side table in the first-floor bar of Jaseer Hotel, a desultory watering hole near Smith's house. We are the only customers. Smith is having chicken biryani with Kingfisher beer.

'The flats look drab and the area has no character. But now I'm used to it,' he says, gesturing at the window that looks on to a Ring Road flyover clogged with buses and autorickshaws. Afternoon sunlight is falling boldly on the old man's wrinkles.

Smith speaks in long sentences as if dictating a book. 'In all, I have had intense relationships with forty-five women in my life. Twenty lived in GB Road.'

I pour more beer into Smith's mug.

Since Smith had no email, I had to call various people before I got his mobile phone number. On the phone, he sounded withdrawn. I could hear a woman's voice in the background. He said he lived in Mayapuri and would not mind meeting me at some bar near his place.

'I arrived in Delhi in the sixties and soon started visiting the kothas. My colleagues in the *Statesman* would tease me,' Smith says. He is wearing a light-brown cardigan and his grey corduroy trousers are frayed.

'I would not go alone to GB Road. We were young and scared of the place. We had the guts to go there only in a group of three or four. Then we would just barge in like scared cocks. What if somebody saw us in the red light area? What if a cop slaps us? You never know what might happen in such places, man.

'I did nothing the first time I went to a kotha in GB Road. But my friends did. And when we were leaving the kotha, a woman—she must have been the malik—politely asked us, pointing her finger at us one by one, "Sir, are you done with your fucking? Sir, are you done with your fucking? Sir, are you done with your fucking? Sir, are you done with your fucking?"'

Smith asks for another bottle of beer.

'The dancing usually started at about seven in the evening. I observed that many respectable and well-to-do people of Delhi attended the *mujra*. They would come wearing garlands made of fresh chameli flowers. These garlands were bought from old prostitutes to whom no one would go and who had been reduced to wretchedness. These hags would take up their places in the dark staircases of the kothas and the customer would buy garlands from them on their way up. In 1963, I took The *Times*'s India correspondent, Peter Hazelhurst, to GB Road for a story and he gave 100 rupees to one such woman.

'The dancing girls danced to film songs, which were usually of the old-world kind: a woman longing for love and how no one is faithful to her. Those kinds of lyrics. As the girls danced, customers would tempt them to come closer by showing rupee notes. We customers sat on mattresses on the floor.

'The best dancing girls came from Firozabad, the town near Agra famous for its bangles. In those times, there was no TV. The dancing girls provided the entertainment.'

Smith had spent his childhood in Agra, where his family's home was about a hundred yards from a church.

'My family had been living in that house since 1869, the year Mahatma Gandhi was born. In 1948, there was a big scandal because of a dancing girl. There was this aristocrat called Chawal Walle Nawab—very rich man, very good family—who fell in love with a dancing girl. Back then every dancing girl was called a *randi*. The nawab would visit this randi almost daily. His wife got upset. One day they had a squabble. The nawab took out his pistol, the wife dashed out of the mansion and ran towards a nearby police station. The nawab followed her and shot her dead inside the police station. He was hanged. The randi, I was told, went on to have many other affairs with many other men.

'In those days, GB Road was not as unruly as it is now. The girls, the dancing girls, especially, used to be very charming and they were so beautiful, so romantic and coy. They looked like film stars. They wore saris. When you offered them money, they would playfully lift the *pallu* of their saris and cover your face with it. Sometimes they would dance especially for you. Now everything has changed, the women wear jeans. In those days they had innocence written all over their faces. They seemed to have come from good families.

'Almost all of them grew up in villages. Most hailed from central India. Many had been kidnapped. Two of the many women I often visited even asked me if I would be able to post a letter written by them to their relatives. I agreed, but I have no idea what became of them.

'It is too long ago but let me see . . . there was Ameena. Yes, Amna, Zubeida, Shakeela, Radha, Shikha, Rosy. Rosy was a Christian. All of them yearned to go back to their families, and live a respectable life with somebody who would marry them. They had fond memories of their brothers, sisters, mothers, especially, and even of their stern fathers. Shakeela, I remember, said that her lover who lived in her neighbourhood had kidnapped her and brought her to Delhi. She was sold in GB Road.

'The dancing rooms were beautifully done. There were mattresses and cushions on which one could recline while watching the women dance. There were Persian carpets on the floor and chandeliers hanging from the roof with hundreds of bulbs. In the evening, when it was close to the time for customers to arrive, there were these two old chowkidars on the verge of retirement. They acted like pimps. Armed with a lathi each, they would knock at the door of every kotha, calling out to the girls. In one kotha, they might say, "You still haven't got ready, randi? Customers are waiting." In another kotha, they would shout, "You are still applying kajal! Quick, it's time for business." Once, just as a woman entered the dancing room dressed in sharara and kurta for the evening, one of the chowkidars said, "Pull down your kurta. You want to show your ass?" These two men would be paid a little commission by every kotha.

'There were cubicles in each kotha, beyond the dancing room. You just had to point to a girl you liked and you would be immediately directed to a cubicle. There would be a wooden single cot inside. The girl would bolt the door and expect you to undress her. These women were very experienced in what they did but I don't think they seemed to get any pleasure out of the sex act. I spoke to one of them and she said, "Most men who come to us are so unclean. One doesn't shave, another smells bad . . . "

'Then there were the customers who liked sadism. They would inflict physical pain on the poor girl and often hurl obscenities at her. And yet, there were occasions when someone really good-looking, sympathetic and sincere would come along. Sometimes, if he became a regular customer, a girl would fall in love with him. But, tell me, is there any future for relationships that are made in GB Road?

'The irony is that one could not bring a relationship made there to fruition. The men had their hang-ups. How could they make a GB Road woman their girlfriend?

'One dancing girl called Zahira told me a strange story. A wrestler came to her kotha and asked her to take him to a cubicle. He then locked the door, undressed himself and then undressed her. He had brought one *seer* of mithai.

'He sat down naked in front of her, put one mithai inside her, then took it out and ate it. He then took another mithai, put it on his penis and gave it to her to eat. He continued doing this until the mithai was finished. After that he opened a bottle of beer, poured some in the cap, poured into her and then sucked it out. He kept doing this for ten minutes. Finally, Zahira protested that the beer was burning her so he drank the rest of the beer from the bottle and left. Mind you, the wrestler did not have intercourse with Zahira, but he did pay.'

'How much would the women be paid?' I ask.

'About twenty rupees for sex. But all that money would go to the malik. If a girl wanted to earn extra money, she had to depend on tricks. For example, once a girl had locked the cubicle and she and the customer took off their clothes, she would start shouting something like, "Help, help. This barbarian is biting my nipples." The pimps would then knock wildly at the door and the girl would stop only after you had given her five rupees. Some of that money would also go to the pimp. The girls would say anything to get money out of you.'

Smith's phone rings. 'Yes, I'm coming. No, I'm alone. Yes. Will be back in fifteen minutes.' Turning off the phone, he says, 'That was my wife. I have to go home.'

'Can I accompany you?'

WE ARE ON A BUS. 'My father's great-great grandfather was Colonel Salvador Smith. He was one of the chiefs of Maharaja Daulat Rao Scindia. He was an Englishman.'

We got off at our stop, the Metal Forging Factory. Crossing the highway, Smith holds my hand as we weave through the traffic.

Walking down Arya Samaj Road, we turn right into Vatika Apartments. Stray puppies are napping under the parked Marutis and Indicas. The middle-income-group apartments are all painted yellow. Clothes are drying on balconies. The benches in the park have been taken over by overgrown grass. A woman watches us from her terrace.

'I first met Alvina in Agra. Since our families were against the marriage, we came to Delhi and exchanged vows in the Lodhi Road church.' We climb the stairs. 'Now I have five children: Enid, Bunny, Tony, Minnie and Rodney. Rodney has Down's syndrome.

'Here's my flat.'

The house is in chaos. The walls are being whitewashed. The sofa has been dumped on the terrace. The dining table has been pushed against the wall. The bed is covered with a white sheet. Framed portraits of Christ are arranged on top of one another on a lounge chair. 'Shh, stay here,' Smith says. He goes into the kitchen. One minute passes. He comes out with a sheepish smile, followed by Mrs Smith. She has grey hair and dark brown skin, and she is wearing a yellow floral-print gown. She is very short.

A pause, and Mrs Smith says, 'Our house . . . you can see for yourself . . . I don't know where I can ask you to sit.'

'Perhaps I can take you to my library,' Smith says.

The room is empty except for a dusty aluminium bookcase, taller than Smith. One shelf has books by Arthur Conan Doyle, Robert Louis Stevenson, Stanley Lane-Poole, Matthew Arnold and H. Rider Haggard. Their spines are covered in dust. Another shelf has books by Smith: *Tales the Monuments Tell*,

Glimpses of Delhi, Lesser-Known Monuments of Delhi, Delhi Vignettes and *The Delhi That No-one Knows*. The top shelf is piled with cardboard boxes.

'What is inside those boxes?' I ask.

'My latest book. It was published last year. The publisher sent me the unsold copies.' I take *Jasmine Nights and the Taj—A Romantic Novel* out of the box. Smith dusts it with a cloth, saying, 'It has some GB Road in it.' He gives it to me. 'This is for you.'

I'M IN SABIR BHAI'S ROOM, flipping through Smith's novel, until I stop at this page:

Sitara applied kajal to her eyes, turned around and looked at her lips, put a rose in her hair and smiled to see the effect of her pearly teeth and the lipstick. She then walked into the hall where the musicians were already seated. But just then she happened to glance towards the staircase and saw the old woman who always stood there with a garland in her hand. Her name was Banjo Bai and fifty years ago she was the one who had stolen the hearts of countless lovers. But youth and beauty had fled and in their place now was a toothless hag with lice in her snow-white hair and a stink from her filthy clothes. Sitara tossed a coin towards her and she gratefully accepted it with a prayer for her benefactress.

'What are you doing, Soofi Sahib?' Sabir Bhai enters, talking in his peculiar singsong voice.

'Bhaijaan, I wonder what GB Road was like a hundred years ago.'

'It didn't exist. A filthy drain flowed here.'

'So, then who made the red light here?'

'The British built it. GB stands for Garstin Bastion. I think he was a commissioner.'

'You mean the British gave Delhi its red light area?'

'No, no, no. The red light area was earlier in Chawri Bazaar, near Jama Masjid. GB Road came up around the country's Independence. The sex workers came here that year. I'm told things used to be different in Chawri bazaar. The women didn't dance to cheap film songs but to the thumri and dadra of classical music. You know Saira Banu?'

'The actress? Dilip Kumar's wife?'

'*Haan*, her mother's kotha was in Chawri Bazaar.'

'Bhaijaan, tell me more about Chawri Bazaar kothas.'

'But I was of Masoom's age then, and, anyway, I was not living in Delhi.'

I MEET SMITH AGAIN.

'I managed to only hear about the twilight years of Chawri Bazaar kothas. If I remember correctly, I'm talking of the times before Independence. You felt as if you were in decadent Mughal times. The women were very courteous. The way they greeted you, asked about you—it was not crude. They were very sophisticated.

'The cubicles were not small and dingy, stark and forbidding, like the ones you have in GB Road. The rooms were divided into spacious cubicles. Sometimes you had a double bed where you could poke your girl. Why, you could even have great food there. While lying in the arms of their women, customers would call out from the balcony and vendors came up to sell their biryani. Some men insisted on getting their kebabs from the Jama Masjid area.

'The burly Pathans from the mountains were quite infamous among the Chawri Bazaar women. The general impression was that they enjoyed sodomy. There was this pathan who had a cat. He was living near the Jama Masjid. Soon, the rumour spread that the pathan was regularly doing it to his cat. Some woman put two and two together and figured out why that neighbourhood was called Ballimaran. 'Billi' is cat and 'maran' is banging. Ballimaran!

'In Chawri Bazaar, there were four categories of women. The lowest of the low was the *domni*. Then came the *bedni*. Then the *tawaif*. And at the top was the randi.

'When a randi took a tonga ride in Daryaganj, people would swarm to the roadside to have a look at her. Randis would leave their kothas only in expensive saris and shararas. And mind you, young man, a randi had values. She would not have sex with anybody. She would be kept by a nawab or some such rich man and she would be his alone. Only after that relationship ended would she look around to form another attachment. People from high castes and rich families sent their sons to randis so that they could learn etiquette.'

'Like how to make love?'

'Not only that. There are other important things, too. Like, how to talk, how to behave in society. Even . . . let's say, how to eat paan in the correct manner.

'The betel leaf was rolled into a ring-shaped *gillori* made of silver, and only then was it offered. If you were unsophisticated, you would put the whole thing into your mouth and perhaps hurt your tongue. But if you were stylish, you would first remove the silver clasp elegantly and then insert the paan in your mouth.

'The tawaifs, on the other hand, were not expected to be faithful to one man. They were friendly to anyone who offered them money. If a man came to a tawaif every day, she would seemingly belong to him, talking only to him, sitting with him, sharing his meal. But if he stopped coming, she would quickly pick another man. Actually, come to think of it, it was a very fine line that differentiated the randis from the tawaifs. Even bednis, though not so sophisticated, had some delicate manners. Some of these bedni women had a tendency to pick and choose their customers.

'The lowest, the domni, entertained anybody with no questions asked. The thing that was said about them was "Go to a bedni, give her two rupees, lift her legs on your shoulders, do your act and take your leave." You know what I mean. Domni women were considered dirty. In Chawri Bazaar, their quarters were said to be the shabbiest. While other women would excuse themselves to wash after the act and come back clean to spend more time with you, a domni would not care to even wipe herself before taking another customer.

'That race of randis and tawaifs is gone. For them dancing and sex were not the only performances of the night. They indulged in conversations with you. They spoke in chaste Urdu and recited the poems of poets like Ghalib, Daag and Sauda. In the old times, husband and wife would have paan after the act. A tawaif would similarly bring paan for you. In their kothas, the cooks would be busy all night making kebabs, mutton biryani, aloo *saalan* and *shahi tukda*. No customer would be allowed to go without a proper meal. Can you imagine that now?'

THE TRAIN COMES TO A HALT. The doors slide open. Not many passengers get out. At almost 100 feet below ground, the Chawri Bazaar metro stop is the deepest in Delhi. Maybe because it is noon, the station is not crowded. The clattering hum of the escalators echoes off the grey walls. After climbing three floors, I step out into Chawri Bazaar. The sanitized world of the metro bears no connection with the chaos outside: overhanging wires, sleeping dogs, shouting food vendors, and rows and rows of rickshaws tinkling their bells. The building that faces the metro station looks at least a century old. It is made of wood, painted green. The terrace upstairs has carved balustrades. Was it once a kotha?

The street is lined with shops selling wire mesh, perforated sheets, copper rods and brass pipes. I buy a cone of roasted peanuts from a vendor and sit down on the stairs of the station. A mother is cooing to an infant in her arms. Two labourers rest on gunny sacks, looking listless. A driver is taking out metal rods from his Matador. A constable is chatting to a shopkeeper. He spots me and comes over.

'What do you want?' he asks.

'I'm . . . I just want to see Chawri Bazaar.'

'This is Ajmeri Gate Bazaar. Chawri is over there,' he says, pointing to the right.

Dust and fumes. The circular centre of the Chawri Bazaar chowk is the transparent dome of the underground metro station. A few beggars are dozing on the periphery. Labourers are having a lunch of dal and rice. A man in tattered clothes is sitting beside a bag of rubbish he has collected for the day. Vikrams—large autorickshaws used for heavy loads—are parked near the sleeping beggars. The chowk is jammed with cycle rickshaws. One has a woman in a blue Benares silk. She is wearing an expensive-looking black overcoat. The skyline is taken over by hoardings advertising wire mesh. Most of the buildings look new but I spot two old mansions. One has thick columns on its balcony. The other has intricate floral designs carved on its balustrade.

I walk towards Chawri Bazaar. Its arcade is exactly like that of GB Road. The shops sell doorknobs. Above one shop are dainty semi-circular balconies jutting out from the second floor. But the balconies have been filled up with concrete. Was this the place where the girls stood to woo customers?

In his book, *The Last Mughal: The Fall of a Dynasty, Delhi, 1857*, William Dalrymple writes:

On such nights, when [emperor Bahadur Shah] Zafar retired relatively early, many of the princes would head out into the town as things began to wind down in the Fort.

Some might have assignations in the kothis of the Chauri Bazaar, where lights and the movement of dancing could be seen from behind the lattices of the upper floors, and the sounds of tabla and singing could be heard from as far away as Chandni Chowk. 'The women deck themselves in finery,' noted one visitor, 'and position themselves at vantage points to attract the attention of men, either directly or through pimps. An atmosphere of lust and debauchery prevails here and the people gather at night and indulge themselves.'

There are no signs of that world. An old vendor in a dhoti–kurta is serving a plate of *chhole–kulche*. He squeezes the lemon on to the chhole but his hands are shaking. The lemon wedge falls to the ground.

Dalrymple continues:

The beauty and coquettishness of Delhi's courtesans were famous: people still talked of the celebrated courtesan Ad Begum of a century earlier, who would famously turn up stark naked at parties, but so cleverly painted that no one would notice: 'She decorates her legs with beautiful drawings in the style of pyjamas instead of actually wearing them; in place of the cuffs she draws flowers and petals in ink exactly as is found in the finest cloth of Rum'. Her great rival, Nur Bai, was said to be so popular that every night the elephants of the great Mughal umrah completely blocked the narrow lanes outside her house, yet even the most senior nobles had 'to send a large sum of money to have her admit them . . . whoever gets enamoured of her gets sucked into the whirlpool of her demands and brings ruin on his house . . . but the pleasure of her company can only be had as long as one is in possession of riches to bestow on her.'

Five labourers are sitting on a bench, listening to *Sheila ki jawani* on the radio. Would they know of any house or a shop that was formerly a kotha?

IN ONE OLD RUN-DOWN MANSION, the wooden strips on the upper floor have fallen off to reveal stencilled balconies. I enter through its imposing wooden gateway. A Gurkha guard points to a notice board:

NO ENTRY

PRIVATE

TRESPASSERS WILL BE PROSECUTED

An old bearded man wearing a brown skullcap beckons me from across the road. Clad in a checked salwar suit and a pea-green cardigan, he is sitting in a sunny spot. Behind him is the staircase to a mosque. 'Rafu master' Mohammed Nooruddin is a tailor who mends torn clothes. He has been sitting at this place daily for forty years. He seems to be over seventy years old.

'What are you looking for?' Nooruddin asks.

'Chacha, Chawri Bazaar used to have kothas before they moved to GB Road.'

'I remember, but first you must have chai,' he insisted, and got some from a stall across the road.

'Those women were banished from the Red Fort's durbar but they were still considered very civilized,' he says. 'Great families would send their sons to learn from them, like how to talk to the elderly, how to salute and greet nobles in the Red Fort and other such things. The women would talk with great

elegance to these boys. They never danced or sang, or stood on the balconies.'

The elderly man seems to remember only the undebauched in Chawri Bazaar.

'Those were very different times. You know hookahs? Their pipes used to be very long. When a young man conversed with a woman, and had the urge to smoke, he called out to the hookah-wallah from the balcony. The hookah-wallah would sit outside on the road while a servant carried the long pipe all the way up to the first floor of the kotha. And the hookah-wallah never specified a fee. He would take whatever was given to him. That was how things were done.'

Closer to the Jama Masjid, shops selling doorknobs and wire mesh give way to wedding-card stores. The card business started in Chawri Bazaar during the 1970s. A wide range of cards are sold here in colours ranging from maroons and purples to whites. One store owner tells me the bazaar has more than 500 card shops. Another claims that it is Asia's biggest wedding-card market. This is no longer a place fit for the dancing girls.

At night, they dance

THE STAIRS OF THE KASHMIRI BUILDING, its back to the railway tracks, are lit with electric lamps. The white tiles on the wall are stained with betel juice.

On the first landing, a dozen men are looking into a brightly lit room. Inside, there are women in bright saris. Three musicians with a harmonium and tabla recline against a wall. They are in kurta–pyjama. A few customers in jeans and leather jackets sit cross-legged. The walls are decked with portraits of Ganesha and Shiva. The large frame at the centre has the garlanded photo of an old woman. A name is written crudely in black ink: Kashmiri Devi.

A middle-aged woman in a purple sari signals me to sit beside her. The girls are facing the customers. Their make-up is light and they look beautiful. Almost all have their saris tied far below the navel and all display ample cleavage. The musicians start playing. The sound is barely melodic; it's rough and raw.

Two girls get up and, walking towards the men in leather jackets, start swaying their hips. The old musician at the harmonium—his mouth filled with paan—begins a Hindi film song from the 1980s.

Wada na tod, tu wada na tod
Meri chadti jawani tadpe
(Don't break your promise, please don't break your promise
My blossoming youth is in agony)

One customer is smoking. Another has a vodka bottle and a Coke can in front of him.

The two girls sway lazily, smiling at each other as if they share a secret. One girl has a Cupid's arrow tattooed on her arm; the other has a flower on her back. In slow motion, they lift their arms, covering their faces, and then flash a glance at the men by suddenly parting their arms.

Now, the rest of the women are singing along; there is no rhythm, and no effort to sing in a chorus. The woman who invited me to sit beside her presents a steel platter of betel leaves. I shake my head. She turns to look at the dancers.

The singing continues.

As it ends, the hostess looks at me, rolls her eyes as if we have just finished watching a virtuoso performance. We nod at each other in satisfaction. She laughs and, leaning towards me, whispers, 'Now you must offer money.' I take out a 100-rupee note. The two dancers are now seated, replaced by another two. The man at the harmonium starts a new song.

Munni badnaam hui, darling tere liye
Munni ke gaal gulabi, nain sharabi, chaal nawabi re
(Munni got a bad name for your sake, darling
Munni's cheeks are rosy, her eyes seductive, her walk regal)

My hostess again turns to me. She taps her fingers, indicating that another 100-rupee note is in order. I open my wallet. It has a 500-rupee note. If I give it to her, will she return the change? If I want to keep sitting, I'll have to give her money after every song. She is now tapping on my shoulders. Embarrassed, I get up to leave.

The song wafts down the empty stairs.

Outside, the corridor is quiet. A few homeless men are sleeping on the floor.

SUSHMA IS SITTING ON THE STAIRS. She is looking ill. 'I've drunk two bottles of cough syrup but it is still not going away,' she tells me. 'You should have seen me last night. I was miserable. The skin under my eyes had contracted. My blood had frozen.'

On the veranda, Fatima is sleeping on the floor. Half-a-dozen bananas are lying on the bench, their skin rotting to black.

Sabir Bhai is sitting on the other side of the bench.

'Soofiji,' he says, 'Masoom is ill.'

Omar enters, saying, 'He's got food poisoning.'

Sabir Bhai adds to that, 'Yesterday, he got gulab jamun and samosas from Shahganj. He was passing latrine throughout the night.'

'That is why I never eat oily things from the street,' I tell Omar. The roaring sound of water being flushed comes from the toilet. Phalak comes out.

'Bhaijaan,' I ask Sabir Bhai. 'What do you know about the dancing girls?'

'That's limited to three or four *jeena*s (staircases). About two dozen madams run dance establishments. Some of these kothas have five women, some have ten, and some even have twenty. During British rule, the kothas had dance licences issued by the government. After Independence, the licences weren't renewed.'

Sushma enters, telling Sabir Bhai that she is leaving for the hospital. He pulls up his lungi, unties a knot on his blue underwear and, taking Rs 250 from a pouch, hands the notes to Sushma.

'Earlier, every kotha in GB held mujras. This building too held dances. Here we had Maya Devi. Now nobody wants to see mujras. Most women have turned to sex work.'

Fatima wakes up, and stares sleepily at the wall in front of her.

'The music and dance have almost ended. Yes, some middle-class people are still interested, but everyone knows that sex happens under the cover of dancing,' Sabir Bhai says, throwing the stub of his Goldflake cigarette on the floor.

'Most dancing girls are from the *bheriya* tribe, whose women have been doing this work for generations. They are from Rajasthan and they are in many red light areas, not just GB Road. There are also many from tribes like *nanti* and *kanjar*. When they grow old, their daughters inherit the tradition. The birth of sons makes the women unhappy.

'Many of these girls have their houses in society. Some own flats, others live on rent. They come here in the evening and leave by one in the morning. Some must have neighbours who know what they do. Others don't. But how does it matter even if they know? It's not like they will give free rotis to the girls.'

THE NEXT AFTERNOON, I return to Kashmiri Building. Sabir Bhai had recommended visiting it in the afternoon, when only old women are present. The girls would still be in their own homes, and the old women would not mind talking to me.

DAYLIGHT HAS DIMMED the artificial brightness of the room I had seen at night when it was lit up with fluorescent lamps, including a chandelier. I see a kitchen beside the door. A boy is making tea. In the room, young women sit together, examining a bundle of salwar suits, each suit packed in transparent plastic. Near the window, a middle-aged man sits on a mat, eating fish curry and rice. Dozens of fish bones are scattered around his plate. A woman in a pink sari gets up and comes towards me, looking meaningfully into my eyes.

'Actually, I'm a writer . . . '

The welcome vanishes from her face. 'So?'

Another woman gets up. 'We are not interested in talking to the media.'

'We don't have time to waste,' the first woman says.

A third in the group raises her head and says, 'Oye, get out.' DOWNSTAIRS, LEANING AGAINST A PILLAR, I watch the traffic jam. The dancing women will not talk. Why should they tell me their stories? What will they get from my book? Nothing.

I'M IN THE DRAWING ROOM of thumri singer Vidya Rao. Employed as an editor in a publishing house, she is a friend who invites me for a home-made meal whenever I feel a little low or a little lost. She shares her second-floor apartment in Mehrauli with her cat Sufi and hundreds of books. 'So glad you've come. Perhaps you could help me,' she says, disappearing into her kitchen. 'I've got too many books. I'm nervous, want to give them away, not all, but most.'

Waving at the book-lined wall, 'I think you forgot to return my Ahmad Ali?' she says. 'Keep it.

'Shall I make you jasmine tea?'

Lying on the living room carpet I look at the bookshelf. Moti Chandra's *The World of Courtesans* is stacked along with *The Courtesan's Arts* by Martha Feldman and Bonnie Gordon. Frédérique Apffel-Marglin's *Wives of the God-King* is about the rituals of the temple dancers of Puri. There is Louise Brown's *The Dancing Girls of Lahore* and Mirza Hadi Ruswa's *Umrao Jaan Ada*. Umrao Jaan, the famous fictional courtesan of nineteenth-century Lucknow, has been immortalized in films.

I take out *Muraqqa-i-Delhi: The Mughal Capital in Muhammad Shah's Time*. A friend had said this book is not available in bookstores. Written between 1738 and 1741, the Urdu-language travelogue by Dargah Quli Khan, a traveller from Hyderabad, is like a guide to the sacred pursuits and wicked pleasures of Shahjahanabad. If one part has respectful sketches of Sufi saints, another reads like an encyclopedia of the city's tawaifs.

In his book, connoisseur Khan informs us that Zeenat's 'well-shaped figure and coquetry helps increase the lust of the people'. Kali Ganga's 'dark complexion is like the black eyes of a doe'. Behnai has mace bearers as servants. Chamani, who 'enhances the eloquence of her conversations with the use of appropriate idioms', has 'crossed the threshold of her youth' but still has access to the emperor.

Preparing pasta for lunch, Vidya calls out from the kitchen, 'If the dancing girls of GB Road will not talk to you, why not talk to their musicians?'

KHWAJA MIR DARD BASTI, or Shakur ki Dandi, is as congested as a slum. Beggars sing, girls play hopscotch, and cats prowl for discarded meat. The sun never enters the narrow alleys, which stay cool in summer.

In 1947, this was a graveyard. Now, according to locals, 9000 people live here. The basti's shabbiness is made starker by the Dr Shyama Prasad Mukherjee Civic Centre, which is on clear view from Sabir Bhai's roof in GB Road.

The basti is home to the *mirasi*s, a community of Muslim musicians who perform at Sufi shrines and in red light districts. Sabir Bhai said that the qawwals and *tabalchi*s (tabla players) who play in the kothas of dancing girls live here. Searching for them, I reach a tomb. Rarely visited, it has the grave of eighteenth-century Sufi saint Khwaja Mir Dard. Goats loiter inside the circular mausoleum. Outside is a butcher's stall with chunks of meat on display. Until a few years ago, the shrine had no roof.

I wander through the labyrinthine alleys and stop at the chai shack of Naved Jamal. A goat enters, too. Naved Bhai tells me that his grandfather was a trader and had a mansion in Farash Khana, just behind GB Road. 'When grandfather's family grew,' he says, 'the haveli was partitioned, then broken to build smaller rooms to fit in married sons. Finally, we were too many, and we had to look for a new place.'

On discovering that I'm looking for mirasis, Jamal says, 'Most of them are moving to Laxmi Nagar.' He is referring to a locality in east Delhi, across the river Yamuna. 'That area is more open.'

SOME ALLEYS IN THE MIRASI PART of the basti suddenly open into cubicle-sized intersections that look to the sky. Goats are tethered to almost every door; passers-by pat them lovingly. Most women come out only in burkas. Sterner than men, they stop anyone new to the neighbourhood. One woman asks me if I'm up to some mischief to evict people so that the basti can be razed and redeveloped as a park.

I climb the stairs of a house. On reaching the first landing, I find half a dozen women watching TV. Spotting me, one of them puts the TV on mute and sits up straight. An old man in brown kurta–pyjama comes down another flight of stairs. His lips are red with betel-juice.

'We don't let in strangers.'

He watches me go down the stairs.

'DO YOU HAVE A PLACE?' Muhammed Sameer asks me. Coffee-coloured, clean-shaven, gym-toned, and of a mirasi family, Sameer runs a car rental agency with his brother. We are on his roof in Mir Dard Basti.

'Yes, I live alone,' I tell Sameer.

'Can I bring a girl? We both can enjoy.'

'You can always go to GB Road.'

Sameer laughs. 'My uncles go there every night.'

'MY FATHER PLAYS THE HARMONIUM. My grandfather used to play it in Chawri Bazaar. I learned the harmonium from him,'

Rehaan tells me. He is Sameer's cousin. We are at Naved Bhai's chai stall.

'I used to go to GB Road every night. But now Abba has stopped taking me there. I'm seventeen and he fears that if I fall for a girl there, our entire clan will be ruined. Not that I show any interest. For two years, I performed there every night with my father. We focused on our job. What kind of people come there, what they say to the women, and what happens there has got nothing to do with us.'

'Ask me,' says Sameer, with a sly smile. 'All sorts of men go there to see the dance. Some are dead drunk. Some have pistols with them. Many are property dealers.'

Rehaan says, 'The customers have seen the world. Many have been betrayed in love. They come to see the tawaifs to forget their life. While watching mujra, they get some relief. Sometimes, there are people who are not married and tend to be lonely.

'The girls, however, enjoy life. They chew on gutkha and smoke cigarettes. At night, they dance; during the day, they talk to their boyfriends on mobile phones.'

'One woman made me her boyfriend,' Sameer says. 'I don't go to the dancing girls since my relatives would recognize me. But I was a regular at number 256, where no dancing happens. Only fucking. There a girl took a fancy to me. We exchanged phone numbers. Since then she never charged me for my fuck-shots.' Rehaan starts laughing. Sameer says, 'If a whore likes a boy, his life is taken care of. She will give him pocket money and, sometimes, if she is particularly caring, she will even get his phone card recharged!'

Rehaan says, 'If her boyfriend is present, the girl won't entertain other customers. Other women will mockingly address the boy as *jijaji* (brother-in-law). Almost every girl in Kashmiri Building has a boyfriend.'

'It's easy to become a whore's boyfriend,' Sameer says. 'I go to Kashmiri Building. A girl dances. I like her and give her money. Now, I visit the building every night, and ask only her to dance. I give her money every night. Soon, we share meals. One day, I become her boyfriend. Rehaan, tell Soofi how a girl fell in love with you.'

'She was not a professional,' Rehaan says, suddenly turning serious. 'Neha had come from Nepal. She was very simple and never cuddled cheaply with any man, never cracked dirty jokes. She liked me. Every evening, when I reached the kotha with my father, she would give me Coke and Uncle Chips. One day, she was wearing a yellow friendship band. When I praised it, she immediately took it off and tied it round my wrist.

'I don't know if Neha misses me. Now I get programmes in weddings and farmhouse parties. Tonight, I'm performing *sufiana* songs at an engagement ceremony in Le Meridian. Come with me?'

'Yes, Soofi,' Sameer says. 'You must go with Rehaan and give me your room keys.'

APART FROM NEW CHARTBUSTERS, there are a few old film songs that have remained evergreen for several decades in the dancing establishments of GB Road. One of them, Rehaan told me, is from the 1972 film *Pakeezah,* a film about a courtesan.

Inhi logon ne, inhi logon ne
Inhi logon ne le leeya dupatta mera
(It is these people, it is these people,
It is these people who have taken away my dupatta)

'I'M THE DESCENDANT of Khwaja Ubaid Ullah Ahrar, the Sufi saint of Tashkent. Babur, the first Mughal emperor, was his disciple. Have you read *Baburnama*? The emperor mentions the Khwaja in his memoirs. It was after obtaining his permission that Babur invaded India.'

Masroor Ahmed Khan lives in a section of what remains of Sharif Manzil, a centuries-old haveli in Ballimaran. Fifteen minutes from GB Road, Ballimaran is, like most places in Shahjahanabad, a dilapidated neighbourhood of crumbling houses, cramped shops and crowded lanes. In the times of the Mughals, it was an upper-crust locality of Muslim noblemen and merchants. I have come to see Khan Saheb because of his haveli. This house, I'm told, hosted mujras when tawaifs lived in Chawri Bazaar.

'I'm a descendant of the first and second khalifa of Islam. We were based in Mecca, from where we migrated to Central Asia to preach Islam. From there, we came to India.'

In the courtyard, a dog barks in front of a woman performing the afternoon prayer.

'Of course, most people remember my great uncle Hakim Ajmal Khan. He was a great scholar of Unani medicine and also a great leader of Muslims.'

A maid enters with a tray of tea and biscuits.

'In the old times, Lala Chunnamal was Shahjahanabad's richest Hindu. We were the richest among the Muslims. We had eleven cars.'

I look around the drawing room. There is a thick carpet on the floor. The walls are covered with paintings and photographs of the family's great men. There is a carved sandalwood etching of the Jama Masjid. A shelf is stocked with books in Urdu.

Following my gaze, Khan saheb says, 'As the family expanded, the haveli was divided into many apartments. Each had a *mardana* and a zenana section for men and women. This drawing room was part of the mardana. We hosted mehfils here. Amid a circle of close friends, tawaifs from Chawri Bazaar were invited to perform mujras. There would be about five courtesans. Their leader was called nayika. The women were dressed in tight churidar pyjamas and lehengas . . . you know, like Meena Kumari in *Pakeezah*. There

were mirasis who played with them. We called them *saajinde*s. The women danced individually or in pairs. While they danced, dried fruits, hookah and cigarettes were passed among the guests. Later, kebabs, biryani and korma were served.

'There were only men in the audience. Our women lived in purdah. They went to the bazaar in draped palanquins, which *kahar*s carried on their shoulders. These kahars were low-caste Hindu men kept by our family. But sometimes during the mujra, our women watched the dance standing behind a *chilman*, a kind of curtain. If you stand behind it and turn off the lights, you can see through it, but the people on the other side cannot see you.'

Khan Sahib gets up to reach the mantelpiece behind my sofa and realigns the two decorative plates. One shows St. Peter's Square in Rome, the other the Eiffel Tower of Paris.

'In old times, most heroines in Bombay had come from red light areas. Saira Banu's mother, Naseem Banu, was a tawaif in Chawri Bazaar. My father said that Naseem's mother, Shamsad Begum, had her establishment somewhere near Namak Waale Phatak. She was very wealthy. Naseem lived with her mother and performed mujra only in front of her man. Saira's father was a famous architect, I think. He went to Pakistan after the Partition.

'Partition came like a tsunami for Sharif Manzil. Many of us went to Pakistan. Those who stayed back had to fight court cases to reclaim our properties that had been taken over by custodians for Hindu refugees. The haveli was returned to the family in the late 1950s.'

We finish our tea.

'I remember watching the mujras in this room. I would sit on my father's lap. Women of the family stood behind the chilman. Back then we had big, round pillows called *gao-takiya* and smaller pillows called *takaini*s. There were no sofas and guests sat on the carpets. Chandeliers hung from the roof. In the evening, before the mujra began, a servant would slowly pull down each chandelier from its brass chains, light the candles and slowly pull the chain on the other side, taking it up to its original height.'

IN SABIR BHAI'S KOTHA, the bulbs are switched on when the muezzin cries out to the faithful for the evening prayer. There are no tawaifs and mirasis. The only music is what comes on TV, or what I hear on Nighat's mobile phone, each time she receives a call.

Kyun paisa paisa karti hai, kyun paise pe tu marti hai
Ek baat mujhe batlaa de tu, us Rab se kyun ni darti hai
(Why do you keep chanting 'Money! Money!'? Why do you love money?
Just tell me this: why are you not afraid of God?)

How old are you?

THE ROOM IS DARK, almost black. The air smells of cold dal. I squint, grope hesitatingly through the empty space with my arms, and before I can take another step, I hear her start talking as if she was simply picking up the thread of a recent conversation. '. . . and they died in the ice flood. The world is no good. It hurts to see so much grief. I have full faith in Jesus. I'm a sinner, God. Just show me a glimpse of yourself. But I tell you He has done a lot for me. But I'm with people in their grief. I don't go to their houses, but I'm with them. I'm saddened over the flood victims. Baba, their houses, their entire houses, went down the ice. Very sorry for the poor people. God, do something for them . . . '

And now I can see her. A band of afternoon light streaming in from the veranda illuminates her profile. Slowly turning her face to me, she continues with her monologue.

'But why me? Listen, go to the slums, there you will find people with stories. Yes, go there.' Her lips are thick, her cheeks are flabby but the most prominent features of her face are the bags under her eyes.

'You are Sunil's mummy?' I ask.

'I don't know when he'll be back, but sit,' she says, pointing to a chair filled with old newspapers. I hesitate. On a closer look, I discover a frying pan and a peeler, too, in a corner of the seat.

'Let me,' she says. She picks up a folded newspaper and uses it to sweep the pan and the peeler on to the floor. The peeler rolls towards the door. Beyond the door a woman sits in the veranda plucking spinach leaves. Another enters from outside the terrace, carrying a red bucket.

This is kotha number 302. It is one establishment away from Sabir Bhai's kotha. I met Sunil last night when he had come to meet Sabir Bhai. A young, slim man, but with a huge belly, he was visibly anxious about something. When I entered, he stopped talking and greeted me without a smile. Then he took the novel I was holding, turned it around, put it down on a wooden stool and left.

Sunil's mother has been running 302 for about two decades. Two years ago, her legs gave way to arthritis. She stopped walking a year later. Confined to her room, she runs the kotha from inside these four walls. The door remains open and she keeps an eye on the customers and the women. Sabir Bhai told me that the mother and son are in a crisis. The GB Road 'mafia' has discovered that the old woman is no longer mobile and they are looking for an opportunity to take over her kotha. They are offering twenty lakhs. But the market price of 302 is about sixty lakhs. The mafia, apparently, does not bargain. Sunil, who grew up in 302, had come to Sabir Bhai for advice. What should his mother do? If they were forced to sell the kotha, where would he and his mother live?

'When a girl gets a customer, I need to be awake, or else they won't give me the money,' the mother says suspiciously. Beside her, a coal stove radiates heat.

'Don't tell me they can fool you,' I reply.

'Shh, it's a bad profession and the times have changed. Earlier, there was honesty in this line.'

A woman enters, saying, 'Mummy, this is Pushpa's.' She hands two fifty-rupee notes to Sunil's mother. The old woman picks up a plastic box from her bed and keeps the money inside. She then pats the bed with her hand as if searching for something. A few seconds later, she takes out a small purple diary from beneath a stack of newspapers. She again pats the bed, searching for her glasses. I pick them up from the table and give them to her. She takes out a Reynolds pen from inside her blouse and makes an entry in the diary.

A woman in the veranda shouts, 'Your mother's cunt!'

'Arré baba,' the old woman bites her tongue looking mildly embarassed and lets out a high-pitched giggle. 'These girls don't know how to behave. I don't like them cussing. By the way, they are very clever, very shrewd. If you aren't careful, they will make a fool of you and you won't even realize it. They lie all the time. Sometimes, you have to use their language on them. But don't mistake me, when I speak cuss-words, it's not from the heart.'

Before I went to meet Sunil's mother, I asked Nighat to tell me about her. We were in the veranda. Sabir Bhai was reading a Hindi newspaper in his room. Nighat was in a red, velvety salwar suit, her hair falling on her shoulders. She was sitting on the bench, waiting for customers. Phalak was breastfeeding her blonde boy openly. I looked away.

'You mean *habshi ki biwi*,' Nighat says. In politically incorrect language, 'habshi' is the Urdu equivalent of 'nigger' and is often used to refer to anything or anyone black. A black sweet-dish, for instance, made of sprouted wheat and sold in Old Delhi is called habshi halwa. 'Sunil's mother got married twice. Her second husband was an African man with whom she had a daughter. She is pure black but very pretty,' says Nighat.

'Is she also in the business?'

'No, the daughter lives in society with habshi ki biwi's other two daughters.'

In GB Road, when a mother wants to keep her daughter away from the flesh trade, she either sends the child to her village or rents a room in some other neighbourhood in Delhi where a guardian looks after the child. Sunil's mother had done the latter.

'But Sunil is not habshi.'

'He's from her first husband—'

Just then Sabir Bhai entered and cut in, 'But when your mother gets a second husband, that man is your father. That is how the world works.'

Nighat nods.

'I think he is the habshi's son,' Sabir Bhai says. 'Only that he has taken after his mother. The daughter has hair as curly as that of an African.'

'If the mafia force her to sell the kotha, where would she go?' I ask.

'She will go into society, to her daughters.'

'Isn't that a good thing?'

'The mafia won't give her much money. Half of it would go towards paying back loans. The rest would be used in marrying off the daughters. What would be left? Nothing! Here, her kotha is not getting good business, just like ours, but at least there is a steady income. You don't have to worry about your chai and roti.'

'What do you think of him?' Sunil's mother asks me, pointing to a framed picture of Christ on the cross.

This is my chance to make a good impression on the woman from whom I want to get another perspective of GB Road, distinct from the tales of the women in Sabir Bhai's kotha. I hope she will provide me a glimpse into the lives of old women in this red light district. I have to bond with her, and Jesus might be of help here.

'It is easy to say that he was the son of God and that he died for the sins of others and that now he is worshipped by millions,' I say, 'but when he was living in this world, only a few people followed him. He was almost alone but he carried on with conviction. And how disappointing it must have been to be betrayed by a close confidant.' The woman nods, pats her hand across her bed and again brings forth a book.

'I read one paragraph daily. The New Testament.'

The book is slim and has a green cover. I riffle through the pages. 'What language is it?'

'Marathi. I was born in Bangalore but I grew up in Maharashtra, in a village near Pune.'

'What did your father do?'

'He worked.'

'Of course, but what work?'

The woman suddenly begins to withdraw from the conversation.

'Whatever work he could find. But why are you asking? Didn't I tell you that I have no stories to tell?'

I look down towards the stove.

'Who sent you? Sabir? Listen, you may come any time and have chai. That's it. I've seen many smart people in my life.'

'Have I offended you, Aunty?'

'Leave now.'

IT WAS A RELIEF to exit Sunil's mother's room. It was unlit, smelly and untidy. Sabir Bhai tells me that she doesn't leave her room because of her legs, except when she has to go to the toilet. She washes herself only once a week and that too in her room. It has been a year since she last went to the balcony of her kotha. She hasn't seen the sky, the street and the crowds since then. The air in her room feels warm and thick with various smells: food, sweat, coal, medicines. When I saw her she was wearing a worn-out nightie with a fading print of orange flowers. Does the old woman change her clothes? Does she brush her teeth? Comb her hair? Since she can hardly walk, who assists her in the toilet? Sunil? How can anybody live for months in that room?

NIGHAT IS SITTING on the bench. She is wearing a grey cardigan and her yellow salwar is rolled up to her ankles. I sit down beside her.

'What happens to a girl in GB Road when she gets old?' I ask.

Nighat smiles and says, 'Soofi, have chai?'

'Come on, tell me.'

'What happens when she is old? Simple, nobody asks for her. Not the kotha malik, not the customers. Men stop coming to her. In GB Road, life lasts as long as youth lasts. A woman starts being considered old when she reaches thirty. At thirty-five, you are done.'

'How old are you?'

'Twenty-five,' she says, looking guilty.

'Look, a woman doesn't suddenly realize she's old the day she turns thirty-five,' she says. 'It could even be before that. Initially, she might not even know. Gradually, it would dawn on her that her old customers are not coming that often. She might see them opting for younger women. But it is also true that some of those old clients would still visit her, not as much as they used to, though. Sometimes, these customers might miss her, thinking of the good times they had with her in the past. They might feel sorry for ignoring her and enjoy a session with her, paying her the usual amount they always used to give her.

'But it is rare for her rates to remain the same. How can that be? Who would give an old woman 200 rupees when the younger lot could be got at the same price? As a woman ages, her rate drops. First, 250 rupees, then 200 rupees, then 150 rupees, then 100, then 80, 70, 50 . . . you know about Kanta Amma?'

KANTA AMMA, who everyone thought was more than eighty, lived in kotha number 282. Having spent her entire life in GB Road, she often said that she could not live anywhere else. With her wrinkles and toothless face, she looked like a grandmother. And yet, Kanta Amma could be seen walking up and down the GB Road corridor, dressed in a petticoat and a kurta, looking for customers. Her rate was Rs 20. Sometimes, customers who could not think of having sex with her would give her the money out of sympathy. She disappeared two months ago. Nobody could figure out what happened to her.

SUNIL'S MOTHER IS LUCKY. She is old but she is a kotha owner. There are seven women in her establishment. Each time one of them has a customer, half of the money goes to Sunil's mother, who keeps it in her plastic box. It is this money that supports her daughters, who live in society, and also Sunil's lifestyle. Sabir Bhai told me that Sunil drinks a lot and has relationships with many women in the area. When I asked if his mother had been a sex worker as a young woman, Sabir Bhai's reply was 'Ask her'.

IT TURNS OUT she has forgotten that our last meeting had ended in my getting the marching orders.

'Come in. You know what? When you first came here—that was not the first time I saw you. Last week, I was thinking of my first husband when I saw . . . you see this wall,' she points to the wall behind the TV. 'I saw a man coming out of that wall and I was . . . Ooo, what is this, God? Am I in a dream? But that man came out of the wall and sat beside me and I was thinking . . . no! I asked this man, "Hello mister, who are you?" And that man had the same face as yours.

'I saw my second husband—he was an African—in the same way. Are you married?'

'No.'

'Listen, I've seen more of the world than you. My advice: don't fall in love. It does not end well. Look at these women. They keep changing their lovers. Better stay alone. Both my husbands were good. God is good. His world too is good. But look at India. So much terrorism.'

'SABIR BHAI, what is Sunil's mother's name?'

'Everyone knows her as Habshi ki biwi. In fact, 302 is identified more with the habshi than anyone else.'

'Who was this man?'

'A Nigerian. He was a criminal character. He died in police custody. Sunil's mother calls herself Rajkumari. Most likely it's not her true name. Women always change their names when they come to GB Road.'

IT IS EVENING. Nighat has a small mirror in her hand. She is putting on lipstick.

'Nighat, do you know anything more about Sunil's mother than the fact that she was a habshi's wife?'

'Her daughter is a habshi.'

'Anything else?'

'She is Christian. These people eat both cows and pigs.'

'Anything else?'

'Why, Soofi! I don't have any business with her. I keep to myself.'

SUSHMA IS STANDING on the roof. The day is ending. I watch her from across a clay pot placed on the balustrade. There are mustard plants growing in it.

'Where are the yellow flowers?' I ask.

'They will come later,' Sushma says. The hair at her temples is going grey.

'Sushma, can I ask you something?'

'Soofi, I won't be cooking arhar dal today.'

'No, I mean are you scared of getting old?'

Sushma suddenly becomes angry. She is looking down at a scene: a pimp from some other kotha is trying to tempt away a man standing before number 300. 'Bastard, leave that man alone,' Sushma shouts. 'I'll fuck your mother.' Turning to me, she says, 'It is because of these bastard pimps that people are scared to come here. *Bhosriwaale.*'

'Yes, bastards.'

'When women get old, Soofi, they have to go down to the street.' Sushma, gathers her thoughts and speaks 'When an old woman can't get customers, she either returns to her family home or starts doing the daily chores of the kotha she lives in. She sweeps the place, washes the clothes and goes to the bazaar to get rations. She gets milk packets for other women's children and beer for their customers. Nothing horrible happens to older women. There is God up there to look after her. When she dies, her body is not left on the road to be picked by the municipality van. We women collect money and organize a proper burial for her, just as one does for a family member.'

'ALWAYS LISTEN CAREFULLY to people who are about to die. They tell you your future.'

I'm with Rajkumari, Sunil's mother.

'When Sunil's father was ill . . . his stomach had grown big . . . he told me I must not live alone. I laughed, "Why not? I have children," and he said, "No, marry again." Well, what he said came true.'

A woman enters. Giving two 100-rupee notes to Rajkumari, she says, 'Mummy, this is Jaya's and this is mine,' and leaves.

'I met Sunil's father in Pune. He used to follow me around when I was out buying vegetables. And you know how I am. I'm not into boyfriends, not like girls today. I kept to myself. I can't say I loved him but he was a nice man.'

'So Sunil's father was not from Delhi?'

'Arré baba, he was from Delhi. He had come to Pune for some work.'

'So you married him and that's how you landed here?'

'Arré baba, what do you mean? Sunil's father was not a pimp who sold me in GB Road. I lived in society with him. He was very rich. His family had horses and a dog. There was a mango orchard. He had many relatives. We had a house across the Yamuna. But he left everything. He said he would start a shop.'

DESPITE ASKING MORE QUESTIONS, very subtly, very cunningly, I could not gather from Rajkumari just how her first husband had lost his fortune. Her conversation was erratic. Her thoughts moved randomly from one theme to another. Sometimes she would snigger while talking about a serious subject—it could be about Christ, child rape or natural calamities. I wanted to talk to her son, but Sunil was never to be seen.

'I ONLY PRAY, "Jesus, give some brains to Sunil. Rid him of whisky. Get him married. Get him a son and he will become a man." And now, pointing her TV remote at me, Rajkumari suddenly heightens the pitch of her voice, 'But don't think ill of him. Sometimes he doesn't drink for as long as fifteen days. You know, I've chosen a girl for him.

'Sultana lives in Mysore. Nice girl. Scared of God. Good values, like me. When I was young like her, I had zero interest in men. God, I was scared of my father. There were so many men who wanted to marry me,' Rajkumari laughs and shake her head. 'Baba, I had no boyfriends. But I had many friends who were girls. I was very close to Charlotte. We were neighbours and we were

always in each other's house. She went to school, I didn't. When she returned home, we'd play *tippori*.'

'What?'

'You never played it? It's very simple. We'd draw five squares on the ground. When it was my turn, I'd hold a small flat stone, make a prayer, call out to Jesus and then throw the stone into one of the squares. Then I'd hop across the empty squares on one foot and pick the stone from its square and hop back to the starting point. Then I'd again say a prayer and throw the stone.'

A woman outside cries out, '*Behen ki lauri*.'

'Charlotte married. But I heard her man left her.'

DESPITE HER FILTHY ROOM, despite her disjointed talk, despite the poor business of her kotha, Rajkumari is no ordinary woman. Her position is the pinnacle that a woman in a red light district can aspire to reach. She is a kotha owner, the malik. One afternoon, Sabir Bhai, himself a kotha malik, helped me make a list of stages that a woman has to pass through before she can become a malik.

She is sold in GB Road.

She entertains customers, earns money and pays back her buyer, with interest.

Gradually understanding the market, she separates herself from the buyer and goes to a kotha of her choice.

She earns without having to worry about sharing it with her buyer. This is her first attempt at an independent existence.

She keeps changing kothas, but if she has saved a good amount of money in the meanwhile, she buys girls and becomes their madam.

She becomes acquainted with moneylenders.

She borrows money and rents a kotha.

A kotha malik never has to worry about getting old.

'THIS LINE IS NO GOOD. Here women are dirty. I have only God as my friend. Whatever I have today, it is because of Him. He is with me. I only wish Sangeeta hadn't died.'

'Was she your friend?' I ask Rajkumari.

'No baba, she was a woman here. She had a small son. And good manners. Nothing like the rest of the women here. She never insulted me with any bad word. You know, she was Sunil's girlfriend,' Rajkumari whispers to me as if she is sharing a secret. 'One day, she fought with Sunil and left us. She went to another kotha and started drinking. I somehow persuaded her to come back. By then, she was addicted to whisky. But I cried and prayed and made her promise never to drink again. And she stopped.' Here Rajkumari makes the sign of the cross. 'Then it all ended. She fell ill and started crying that she had to go home.'

'Where was her home?'

'In Bengal. I said, "Why not? Please go, by all means." But my point was that please, first get well, recover your health. But Sangeeta wouldn't listen. I told her to call her folks to Delhi and offered to send them travel money. But she wouldn't give us her home address and insisted on going instead. I said, "Okay, go." We gave her the money and all that. She went away with her child. I booked her a train ticket to Kolkata. And what's the next thing I heard?'

'What?'

'That she is dead.'

'And the son?'

'God knows,' said Rajkumari, again making the sign of the cross.

SABIR BHAI HAS ONLY one meal in twenty-four hours, at three in the morning. Right now—it is late evening—he is having buttered toast, which Sumaira got from a chai stall downstairs. We are sitting on the veranda. The black-and-white TV in the alcove is switched to a film channel.

'Have one, Soofi Bhai,' he offers me a slice of toast. There is too much butter on it.

I refuse, saying, 'Bhaijaan, you have been living in GB Road for . . . how many years?'

'*Lo*, I've spent almost my entire life here. I have seen things you will never see in society. I have seen the fate of these women. After forty, when she is reaching forty-five, all is over.'

Nighat comes from the kitchen and sits beside me.

'Customers no longer like her. The younger man would say to her face that she looks like an aunty. She can't even return to her village. How can she? She has spent her entire youth in GB Road. If she goes back home and with hardly any money, why would her folks help her? Instead, they might say, "You spent your youth elsewhere? Where were you? What were you doing?" In many cases, the woman is ashamed to return home dreading such questions.

'So they stay on here. When they stop getting customers, they walk up and down the corridor looking for customers . . . to bring them up to the younger women of the kotha. You could say they become pimps.

'Such a woman gets her commission. Sometimes she merely runs errands for the people living in her kotha, like bringing cigarettes for them or, like our Sumaira, getting buttered toast for me from the chai stall or bringing a bottle of Coke for you. They have to justify their worth if they don't want to be pushed out of a kotha.'

Nighat picks up the TV remote. She is changing channels: Star Gold, MTV, Channel V, Star Movies, Zee Cinema . . .

'WHEN I FIRST CAME to Delhi . . . arré baba,' Rajkumari pauses to rest her right hand on her heart and then she giggles. 'I was so excited. But then I discovered it wasn't a great city. Same kind of neighbours, same films, same rubbish.' She sticks out her tongue, holds her ears and chuckles. 'Sensible people don't live in Delhi. It's too crowded, too noisy. I like villages. When I was a child, I would go to my *naani*'s village. There was a river nearby which was called Ganga.'

'But Ganga doesn't flow in Maharashtra . . .'

'The river water was so clean that it was considered as sacred as the water of the Ganga. You could see the stones under the water.'

'And fish?'

'No, the river wasn't deep enough for them though, well, sometimes you could see smaller fish. My naani would wake up at five in the morning and crush grains in a stone *chakki* and that flour would be immediately used in making rotis. Naani's sons farmed groundnuts and whenever I visited her, she would make peanut chutney for me.' Pointing to a slab of Amul butter, Rajkumari says, 'Earlier, people never ate bread and butter. There was more honesty.'

IT IS AFTERNOON. Sushma is sitting on the balcony. Her hair is caked with green paste.

'Soofi, shall I put henna on your hair? Mine is greying. I have to hide the white strands.'

'WHY DID YOU MARRY a man from Africa?' I ask Rajkumari. She is reading her Marathi Bible.

'Africans are black but they can be nice. He was a good man but he would easily get angry, though he never got angry with me. I have a girl from him. I was lucky. Both my husbands were nice to me. Both sometimes cooked for me.' She giggles. 'But I would peel garlic for them.' A pause. 'I was alone after Sunil's father died. Back then Didi used to run this kotha. She was my distant relative. After Sunil's father died, Didi said, "Where will

you go with your small children? Come to my house and help me run this place." And so I came and, arré baba, men won't leave you here alone. And then Didi died and men would come and sit in my room . . . this same room . . . and I wouldn't know what to do, and so I would give them beer and they would be happy. Sometimes sadhus would come and I hoped they would talk about God. Instead, they asked for whisky as an offering for Bhairon Mandir, near the zoo.'

A woman in a torn sari knocks on the door. Where her eyes should be, there are dark hollows. 'I'm from Kolkata, Ma. Give me something please,' she says, in a sobbing tone.

'Why have you come so far?' Rajkumari asks, her lips twitching.

'Ma, he was ill. So we . . . ' The rest of her words are hard to make out. She is crying and saying something in Bengali. Rajkumari opens her plastic box, takes out a ten-rupee note and gives it to her. The woman cries more.

'Ma, my sari is going to bits. Do you have any clothes, ma?'

Rajkumari exclaims, 'Look at my clothes. Look at my bedsheet. I can't walk. I can't bathe. My son takes me to the latrine.'

The woman turns away, still sobbing.

'When I was new here, I was tense all the time. I was harassed by men. Then I saw this African man at the bus stop near Ajmeri Gate. He was black. I later heard that he had a hundred girlfriends. I would often spot him in the area. And one day I teased him saying why he didn't marry at least one of them. He said, "They don't come to marry me. Some come to get their passports made. Some to take a motorcycle ride with me. Some to pass the time." So I asked him "Why don't you marry me?" and he married me.'

I'VE JUST RETURNED from Rajkumari's room. Sabir Bhai is reading an Urdu daily. Phalak is peeling garlic. Imran is sleeping on the floor. 'Today I discovered a plastic bucket under her bed.'

'Filled with water?' Sabir Bhai asks.

'No, it was . . . horrible. All day, if she has to spit—and she spits a lot—she spits into that bucket. If she has to gargle, she spews out the water into that bucket. If she has to wash her hands, she does that in the bucket!'

Sabir Bhai laughs. 'Her legs are useless. She is suffering for her sins.'

'What do you mean?'

'The earlier malik who had invited her to the kotha after her husband's death was very kind to her, but she had no plans to give back the control of the kotha. That malik had heirs. But once the woman died, Rajkumari got rid of them. That she can't move today is because she has been cursed by those people.'

Phalak speaks up. 'If you do bad things, you'll be punished in this world itself.'

'MY SECOND HUSBAND didn't know Hindi. I didn't know Kolo Kolo. It was his language. So we would talk in broken English.'

'What was his name?' I ask Rajkumari.

'He was Mohammedan. His name could have been Akbar, Salman, Khalid, Omar . . . it wasn't any of these names but it was something like these.

'He died in an accident. We buried him in the Muslim graveyard behind the newspaper building in ITO.'

'Where would you like to be buried?'

'I'm Christian. I'm sure Delhi has Christian cemeteries. It is a big city.'

'Start walking, Aunty, and I'll take you for a prayer service to Sacred Heart Cathedral.'

'Why so far? We have a church here in Fatehpuri. There is one in Chandni Chowk, too.'

'We'll go to Fatehpuri then.'

'If only you were my Sunil. He never sits with me.'

NIGHAT IS STANDING at the balcony, with a copy of *Vanity Fair*. I had given it to her last week. She is turning the pages slowly, looking at each picture for a long time. Meryl Streep is on the cover.

Noticing that I'm looking down at the people on the road, who are looking back at us, she says, 'Soofi, I'm scared of turning forty.' She starts laughing. 'See, I'm thinking so much about it that I've grown thin.' A moment later, she becomes serious as if in deep thought and, looking determined, says, 'I know what I will do. I will go home.'

STIRRING AROUND THE COAL in the stove with a wooden stick, Rajkumari says, 'Let the flames die first or they will blacken the bowl.' She has to heat up yesterday's dal for lunch. 'I love freedom. Azadi. I do things of my own will. Nobody can order me. I am old but I have lost nothing. I sleep when I have to. I eat when I want to.'

A rat climbs the table and running up to the bowl, it tastes the dal.

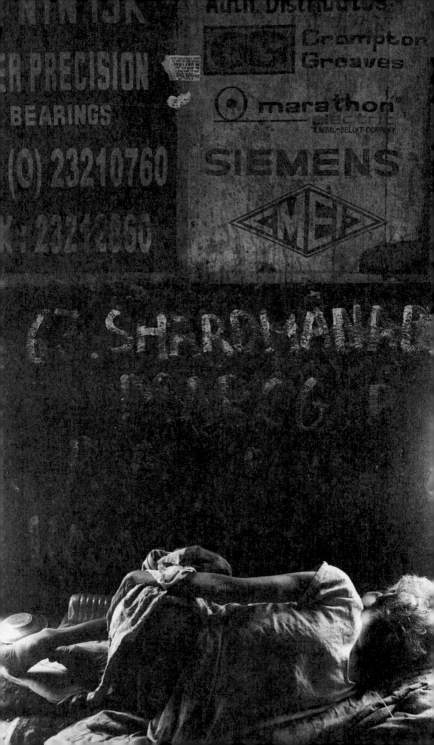

When I'm big,
I'll leave this place

A MOMENT AGO, she was smiling. Now, she is crying. 'Why the tears, Aarti?' I ask her. The eight-year-old shakes her head. Wiping her face, she struggles to smile but starts crying again.

'It is her mother,' whispers Sabir Bhai.

Like other children, Aarti goes to school, plays at home, and fights with her peers in the kotha. Her nose is pierced; her frock is printed with orange flowers. She likes *pakori*s; she hates bananas. She can recite the English alphabet and can count from 1 to 100. Her mother, a woman called Aneeta, has hopes for Aarti. 'I'm waiting for her to grow up so that I can live off her earnings,' she casually told me one evening in the veranda. Aneeta, who arrived in teen sau number three weeks ago, does not talk to me much. She keeps to herself. She does not have a nice rapport with the other women in the kotha. They say that she fights frequently. Sometimes she is violent with customers. I'm asked to keep away from her.

Now Aarti is crying because her mother has been told to move out of the kotha. Aneeta is considered a risk. She is an alcoholic. She shares her living quarters—a large alcove next to the stairs that lead to the roof—with her daughter and a Nepali lover. The man virtually lives on whisky that Aneeta pays for. Sometimes, they have violent fights during which he slashes her arms with

107

his shaving razor. But they always patch things up. It was when Aneeta started robbing her customers at knifepoint that Sabir Bhai gave her an ultimatum. 'If they complain to the police, we will all be in trouble,' he explains.

Aneeta has now decided to shift to number 307. Aarti is unwilling to make the move. They have lived there before. That establishment is very small, crowded and extremely filthy. The women there apparently don't shower for days. Food rots on the floor. Toilets are seldom cleaned. 'Here, Aneeta has the alcove to herself,' says Sabir Bhai. 'There, both mother and daughter will have to live in a small cubicle in which only a single cot would fit.'

Most women in Sabir Bhai's kotha don't want to let Aarti go. 'But who are we to take away a child from her mother?' says Phalak. After a pause, she says, 'Don't be duped by the little girl's innocent looks. She is as cunning as her mother.'

At night, when Aneeta gets drunk, she often gets into a fight with her daughter. Aarti's response to her '*Ek din tu bhi randi banegi*' (One day you, too, will become a whore) was '*Randi, tujhe main jhaapad mar doongi*' (You whore, I'll slap you).

Searching for the mother, I go upstairs to the alcove. Aneeta is peeling potatoes for dinner. Her man is lying on a mat. The hushed laughter of a woman can be heard from some distance. 'Soofiji, do something about Aarti,' Aneeta says. 'Teach her good English.'

In the new kotha, Nighat told me, Aarti's mother would have to entertain her customers in the same bed in which her daughter would have to sleep. 'Can't you let her stay here?' I ask.

'But how can I live without my child?' Aneeta asks. Just then, the lover starts tugging at her kurta. Aneeta turns and plants several kisses on his neck. I go down to the veranda. Sabir Bhai is squatting on the bench.

'Earlier, Aarti would sleep upstairs with her mother and that Nepali man,' he says. 'When Aneeta went out at midnight to get customers, Aarti would be alone with her stepfather. Fearing that he might do something to the girl, we asked Aneeta to let Aarti sleep on our floor with the other children.'

Among the kotha's children, Aarti does not count. 'She's a beggar,' says Masoom, Sabir Bhai's eight-year-old son. The girl is usually ignored and is asked to join in a game only when there aren't enough players. But in a way Aarti is also loved. The women in the kotha take care of her when her mother sleeps during the day. They give her food and a bit of attention.

Is Aarti crying because she fears that she might not receive the same affection in the new place? One day she showed me two sketches she had drawn. One had a doll looking out of a window. It was easy to guess where she got the idea from. In GB Road, most women solicit customers by waving their arms from their balcony windows. The other sketch was a curious combination of a fish and a man. Aarti identified the man as her father. Later Sabir Bhai confirmed that Aarti's biological father, a labourer in Chawri Bazaar, occasionally comes to the kotha to meet her. Once, he had taken her fishing in a lake outside Delhi. Perhaps the memory stayed with Aarti.

According to Sabir Bhai, the labourer is fond of his daughter. Then why can't Aarti's mother move into this man's house? 'She cannot. He lives on the pavement,' says Sabir Bhai. 'Also, once a woman has got used to the freedom of a kotha, she is unable to live in society.'

I walk up to Nighat. Today I learnt she is Phalak's real sister, and that is why the children call her Khala. Nighat is putting white talcum powder on her neck for the evening.

'What is Aarti's future?' I ask.

'Who can say? She will either become somebody or will become like her mother.'

Sabir Bhai says, 'GB Road is a quicksand. Once you get into a red light area, it is very difficult to get out.'

I look for Aarti. She is standing alone in the balcony. By now she has stopped crying. 'What do you want to become when you grow up, Aarti?' I ask.

Her cheeks turning red, she says, '*Kuch nahin*' (Nothing).

AFTER AARTI WENT AWAY with her mother, number 300 was left with four children: Omar, Osman, Masoom and Imran. All are boys. Omar, at twelve, is the oldest. Imran, at two, is the youngest. Their mother is Phalak. Their father is Sabir Bhai. The elder three go to a government school. Omar and Osman, though there is a difference of two years between them, study in the same standard: the seventh. Masoom is in the third. Do the children know what happens in their house? Are they aware how their father earns his living and what the women in their home do? Do they wonder about the men who come to their house every day?

Can I ask the boys?

SHERU DIED ON SUNDAY. The family had two rabbits. He was one of them. The other is called Sherni. Omar explains how it happened. 'It was about noon. Sherni was in the box room, inside her cage. Sheru was sitting on the chair in the balcony. Abbu had gone downstairs. Mummy was in the latrine. There was no one on the veranda. Osman was watching TV inside. The *kala billa*—the black cat—came in through the main door, tiptoed into the balcony and pounced on Sheru. Then the kala billa jumped to the neighbour's roof with Sheru in his clasp. I started shouting. Sumaira ran to the balcony with a wooden pole. Kala billa panicked and released Sheru and ran away. Sheru fell down into the drain. We quickly ran outside and picked him up and washed him. His thigh bone had broken. We planned to take him to the doctor the next day. But he died during the night.'

'What did you do with his body?' I ask.

'We threw it into the dump yard,' says Sabir Bhai. He is smoking a bidi, sitting on the bench.

'What about Sherni?'

'What will she do? She is eating leaves and having fun in life,' says Nighat Khala, sipping her tea.

AMONG SABIR BHAI'S FOUR BOYS, Omar is wiser than his years. He wears black-rimmed spectacles and his hair is short. He reads the Quran daily. He has a prayer bump on his forehead—the mark of faith. When I first met him, about a year ago, he said that he wanted to be a maulana. Unlike Osman, who is always in jeans, or Masoom, who dresses in Spiderman T-shirts, Omar wears loose shirts and trousers. The colours are lighter shades of cream, brown or grey. Today, his costume is almost festive. His white shirt is crisscrossed with navy blue stripes. He is wearing black plastic sandals. We are walking to Chawri Bazaar on an errand. Sabir Bhai has asked him to get the monthly electricity bill photocopied. I sense an opportunity to discuss a matter that I'm uncomfortable raising with him.

'Omar,' I say in a careful, casual tone, as if I'm about to chat about the weather. 'When does a child growing up in GB Road realize what his mother's business is?'

We are walking past a row of hair salons and mithai shops. Flies are buzzing from jalebis to roadside drains and back. I glance at Omar. Have I been rude or cruel? Will he tell Sabir Bhai? Will Sabir Bhai be upset? Will I be asked to stop coming to their kotha?

Omar speaks up. 'When he is fifteen or sixteen years old,' he says, holding my hand. 'When a child is small, he doesn't know what his mother is doing. But later he feels bad, as he realizes that his Mummy entertains men.'

We move to the side of the street to give way to a rickshaw.

'I think I was seven when I discovered that my home was actually a kotha. I saw the things that were happening in my house. We had women sitting on the stairs. They would bring men inside and argue about rates. As I grew older, I realized that this was a wrong kind of work.

'It's wrong. Yes, it's wrong. In a way, it's wrong. In a way, it's right. It's right because the women need money for their families. They have to provide for food. It's wrong because the child suffers for the work his mother does.'

MOTHER PHALAK IS DARK. Father Sabir is dark. Omar, Osman and Masoom are dark. But Imran is almost white. His hair is blonde. Imran, or Immu as he is fondly called, was born of Phalak for sure. She gave birth to him in a municipality-run maternity hospital where most GB Road women deliver their babies. But who is his biological father? He has to be a white man. Was he a customer of Phalak's? Does Phalak remember making love to him? I have never seen a white man in GB Road, except for an occasional backpacker or two who had wandered in from Jama Masjid or Paharganj not knowing this is the city's red light district.

'Immu, shake Soofiji's hands,' Sabir Bhai tells him as I enter the veranda. The child shyly offers his hand to me.

'Now, now, tell him: where is your hair?' Sabir Bhai says in broken English.

The boy touches his hair.

'And nose?'

He touches his nose.

'And eyes?'

He thinks for a moment before touching his left eye.

'And tongue?'

He sticks out his tongue.

'And ear?'

Where is the ear? The boy is puzzled, looks confused and touches his nose. Nighat Khala laughs.

'And ear?' Sabir Bhai repeats.

The boy suddenly touches both his ears. Khala jumps from the bench and kisses his forehead.

'See, he knows English.' Sabir Bhai says.

'He calls his mother "mom",' Khala says.

'He has taken after his people,' Sabir Bhai says, looking proudly at the child.

Imran's people. Who could they be?

I'VE GOT A SECOND-HAND ATLAS for the children. It is evening. Nighat Khala is combing her hair in front of the mirror. Sushma is in the veranda, watching films songs on TV. The volume is on mute. Fatima is lighting agarbattis. Sabir Bhai is performing namaz. Opening the book, I show the world map to Sushma.

'Where do you want to go?' I ask.

'Saudia,' she says, implying Saudi Arabia. 'I want to go to Mecca.'

I point out the city to her and also show her India. Pointing to the United States of America, I ask, 'Why don't you want to go to Amreeka?'

'I don't like it,' Sushma says. 'Maybe New York. It has nice shops.' She laughs. 'It has snow.'

Omar appears. He takes the atlas from me. 'Look at Pakistan,' he says. His fingers move across that country's map, stopping at a black dot that indicates Islamabad. 'Osama bin Laden lives there,' he says.

IT IS EVENING. Sushma is sharpening a knife on the *silbatta*, a stone used for grinding chutneys. Omar enters carrying a bird cage. Inside it is a grey francolin. 'It tastes very nice,' says Omar.

Sushma raises her head, looks at the bird and says, 'It's especially good in winter. Its meat is very warm.'

The knife is sharpened. Omar unlocks the cage. The bird refuses to move. Sushma coaxes it out. 'We bought it only two weeks ago,' Omar says. 'It makes an irritating noise, especially at night.' Sushma holds the bird in her hand. Omar says, 'Now, we'll eat it.'

Sushma asks him to get water. 'It's hot. Let it have a few drops,' she says, placing the bird on the floor. The francolin hops behind a flower pot. Omar brings a plastic wiper and nudges the bird out. Picking it up, Sushma squeezes its neck. Omar hands her the knife. The bird flutters its wings. Just then the muezzin from a nearby mosque starts calling the faithful for the maghrib prayer. The air fills up with his voice. *Allah hu Akbar. Allah hu Akbar.* 'Let's not kill it,' Sushma says, releasing the bird.

'As you say,' the boy says, a little disheartened. The bird hops back into its cage.

OSMAN IS LYING on Sabir Bhai's bed. The TV is on. He is again watching *Dabangg*, his favourite film.

'Not again,' I say, lying down beside him, snatching the remote from him.

We browse through channels. 'I want to listen to new movie songs,' I say.

'Come on, Soofi,' Osman says, taking the remote from my hands. 'You have to watch *Dabangg*.' The movie was a blockbuster. The local cable operator plays it almost every other evening. Osman hasn't grown tired of it. Khala has told me that he dances very well to the film's chartbuster song, '*Munni badnam hui*', but he is too shy to perform in front of me.

'Osman, if you get a free ticket to any foreign destination of your choice, where will you go?' I ask.

'Umm,' Osman thinks for a minute before saying, 'London. I want to see the London Bridge and they have a big clock tower there. I saw it in my schoolbook. I want to see that and I also want to play in the snow. There I will have dinner in a good hotel.'

'What will you have for dinner in London?'

'Chicken, fish . . . and I want to make friends in London. Somebody who works in a big company or is a manager in a big hotel. I want to get a friend who loves me more than my own brothers.'

GETTING OFF THE RICKSHAW, I enter the corridor in GB Road. Women are standing at the entrance to the stairs of number 300. I notice a new woman among them. Very thin, she is in a red top and blue jeans, the legs of which are rolled up to her knees. She doesn't know me and, mistaking me for a customer, she says, 'Come, talk to me.' The other women laugh and tell her that I'm not a client. She moves aside. I walk up. On the first landing, I find Phalak sitting in a corner. She is feeding Imran. Phalak greets me and does not try to hide her breasts. I try not to see them.

'I DON'T LIKE GB ROAD,' Osman says. We are on the rooftop. Sushma is chopping spinach. Osman is trying to fly a kite. 'It's dirty. It's so dirty, so very dirty that everyone falls ill here. You get dengue here.'

'I want to get away from here,' says Osman. 'I want to go to a *grihasthi*.' Grihasthi, 'household' in Hindi, is a magic word in GB Road. Before I started coming here, I never appreciated the true worth of a normal household. For most sex workers, life in a grihasthi is the ideal one aspires to. Life there is respectable, one knows one's father, and a woman does not sleep with unknown men, and there is no poverty.

'You can't study here without getting disturbed,' Osman says. 'Here people snatch money from you. Every day there are new fights. Customers get drunk and beat the women. Sometimes I

116

get scared. I want to study so that I can be a good man. I want to take my *ammi* and my *abbu* out of this place. I will take care of them in the grihasthi.'

Explaining his understanding of grihasthi, Osman says, 'It's a place where everything is good and peaceful. You can concentrate on your studies. There is no fear. Nobody can beat you. There are flats and parks. You can make good friends there and you can bring them home. I cannot bring my schoolfriends to my home. I'm ashamed. I have to make excuses when they ask me if they can come to my house.

'If we bring a classmate here, our reputation will be ruined. My friends and teachers will be disgusted. They would know that I live in GB Road.

'When my classmates ask me where I live, I say Farash Khana,' he says, referring to a neighbourhood close to GB Road.

HE IS OLD, must be in his sixties, but he strongly resembles Imran, especially in the shape of his lips. 'He was our very good friend,' Omar says, showing me this passport-size black-and-white photograph of a white man.

So this man must be Imran's biological father.

'He was very fond of us. Sometimes when he saw us in Pathani kurta and pyjama, he would hug us and cry.

'I don't know where he is now. He hasn't come here since Imran was born.'

We both continue looking at the photograph.

'James was from Amreeka. He was working in India. I don't know if he is still in Delhi but I have his phone number. But I haven't heard from him since the time he stopped coming. When I dial his number, a voice says the number does not exist.'

GOVINDA LIVES IN NUMBER 298, on the floor below Sabir Bhai's kotha. His mother ran away from GB Road when he was a toddler, leaving him behind. He is seven and he doesn't go to school. Once I met him on the stairs and asked him his name. When the kotha malik, Mallika, who is Govinda's self-appointed guardian, came to know about it, she gave him a beating for talking to me. Masoom tells me that Govinda is frequently beaten. Perhaps that is why he looks so hardened. His front tooth is broken. His hair is cropped close to the scalp in the army style. I have never seen him standing still. He is always shouting, running, just beyond one's grasp. For the moment, he has become great friends with Masoom, which is surprising since Masoom is a very quiet child who is happiest when he is alone.

'How could a mother abandon her child?' I'm talking to Sabir Bhai.

'I don't know about Govinda's mother,' he says, 'but I know many women who ran away from GB Road, leaving behind their children. Such women never adjust to life in the kotha. They are always wanting to escape. So, when a customer comes, establishes a relationship with a woman and tells her that he will marry her and take her into society where she can live like a wife, she agrees to leave her world for a new life. In most cases, the promises are false. The man will take her to another city where she would probably be sold into that city's red light area. But the woman doesn't know that and she willingly leaves her kotha, and her child, for her man.'

'But why does she leave her child?'

'Most kotha maliks are insecure about their women running away from their kothas so they keep a tight leash on their children, thinking that a woman won't have the heart to flee without her baby. But sometimes a woman gets so desperate that she secretly runs away with her client, leaving behind the child, hoping that he would be taken care of. It is just helplessness.'

Masoom comes cycling into the room. Govinda is sitting behind on the carrier, holding a toy machine gun.

'Sometimes, even if a client truly loves a woman, he sets the condition that he will marry her only if she agrees to come without the child. There have been instances when a woman returns to her village for good but does not take her child. After all, her people should not come to know what she was up to in the city. Questions would be asked if she appeared with a child.'

'They beat Govinda badly,' informs Omar. We are walking to Farash Khana to have *gole paapes* from the bakery. By 'they', he means Govinda's self-proclaimed mother and brothers. 'Mother' is the kotha malik and the brothers are the woman's two sons. 'They beat him with a wooden pole. Sometimes they slap him and, at least once a month, when he is being very naughty, they burn him with hot spoons.'

'But his mother is not cruel,' Omar says. 'She gives him money to buy toys.'

Until a month ago, Govinda went to school. Then one day he did not return at his usual time—5 p.m. When it got dark, the kotha madam started weeping. She cried and howled and walked down the arcade below several times calling out for Govinda, asking people, 'Please bring me my son! Please look for him.' They were scared to report the disappearance to the police because then questions could be asked about Govinda's real mother. At 8 p.m., Govinda arrived on his own. After school, he had gone to the New Delhi Railway Station to watch trains and have pakoris. On spotting him, the kotha madam stopped crying and got ready to give the boy a thrashing. But the other women of 298 shielded him from the blows, promising the mother on Govinda's behalf that he would never disappear like this again.

On returning from Farash Khana, I find Govinda standing outside the kotha.

'Have paape,' I say, offering him the round bread.

'Soofi, don't,' Omar pushes me upstairs. 'If you talk to him, he'll again be beaten.'

As Nighat makes chai for me—it goes very well with paape—Omar says, 'Every woman in 298 loves Govinda. They take turns to seat him on their lap. If one woman gives him twenty rupees to get toffees, the other buys him clothes.'

THIS IS THE FIRST TIME in the living memory of middle-aged Delhiites that it has rained on Eid-ul-Fitr, the day that marks the end of Ramzan, the month of praying, fasting and cleansing the soul. We are attending the morning namaz at Shahi Idgah, the seventeenth-century mosque built specifically to perform Eid prayers. Sabir Bhai is in a white shirt and a green, checked lungi; the boys are in all-white pathani salwar suits. They are all wearing dark brown astrakhan caps, especially taken out for the occasion.

The Idgah mosque is a vast ground landscaped unevenly with stone slabs, bare earth and overgrown grass. Dating from the times of a later Mughal emperor, the western wall that faces Mecca is a simple structure with unimposing domes and battlements. Sabir Bhai spent Rs 30 on a rickshaw to come to Idgah. 'Jama Masjid is for the Friday Jumma prayers,' he says. 'For Eid prayers, I come to Shahi Idgah every year.'

The sky had been overcast since daybreak, and most worshippers were resigned to the possibility of it raining in the middle of the special namaz. That is exactly what happens. As the ground fills with people, it starts drizzling. A few minutes after the imam begins the prayers, the mild shower becomes a downpour. Umbrellas are opened, plastic sheets unrolled, but the prayers continue. The faithful kneel down, touching the ground with their foreheads, stand up and then again kneel. The rain does not stop. After the prayers, Masoom tells me, 'Allah wanted to test his believers, if they would come for the prayers in the rain or not. That is why he gave us this weather.'

'SOOFI, SAY HELLO to my son,' Phalak tells me. Imran is looking up, his right arm stretched out towards me. 'He's so happy to see you,' the mother says. I want to ask her about James, the American who had fathered the child.

Carrying him, I move to the veranda and sit beside Sabir Bhai. 'Imran is so white, so smart,' he says. 'Last year, I had gone to Kanpur with him and Phalak. It was May, very hot. When we were returning by train, Imran started crying because of the heat and he just would not stop. I was very worried. He is so fair that I feared somebody would suspect we were kidnapping some rich man's child.' Sabir Bhai starts laughing. 'We'll get him admitted into an English-medium school.'

OMAR IS POLISHING HIS SHOES. Imran is trying to polish his feet with another brush. Osman and Masoom are playing football, with the tin cover of Cherry Blossom shoe polish as the ball. Govinda is standing at the door. For the first time I see him still and quiet. Suddenly, Osman asks me, 'Soofi, you have a laptop?'

'Yes.'

'Which one?'

'Apple Mac.'

Not impressed, Osman says, 'You should get Samsung. It's a very good company. My classmate, Nitish, has a laptop. It is his father's. He once took me to his house and showed me how it works.'

'He didn't let you use it?'

'But his father was there. Nitish is very nice. His father works in the government. They live in the railway quarters near Minto Bridge.'

'Has he come to your house?'

'No.'

WE ARE LOOKING FOR JAVED SIR. Omar and Osman have brought me to their school on Mata Sundari Road. According to a government scheme, Muslim children from poor households are given Rs 750 about four times a year. Javed sir, who is the school's Urdu teacher, is responsible for handing out the money. Today is Saturday and there are no classes. Javed sir is supposed to be in the staff room but no one is there. We sit on a wooden bench, waiting for him to arrive. The school is ten minutes from GB Road but it feels like we are in another country. The ground is paved with bricks and there are trees everywhere. 'That's *shehtoot*,' says Osman.

'And that's jamun,' says Omar. The wall outside the staff room is painted with the message:

THE THREE JEWELS OF LIFE ARE COURTESY OF MANNERS, GENEROSITY OF HEART AND RECEPTIVITY OF MIND.

Feeling far away from the world they live in and to which they will shortly return, the boys seem to be experiencing a strange surge of freedom. They speak their mind without any hesitation. 'Why couldn't have Abbu gone elsewhere?' Osman complains. 'He could have found some other work, not this work.' A teacher appears from another room and gives his empty jug to Omar, asking him to fill it up from the water cooler across the ground. Omar gets up. Watching him cross the ground, Osman says, 'Abbu could have set up a shop.'

'How would he have arranged the money?' I say.

'He could have got a bank loan or borrowed money from a relative, but Abbu did not do that and he came to GB Road instead. He says that there is safety in GB Road—that the police are present all twenty-four hours of the day.'

Omar comes back. 'Sharma sir says Javed sir is not coming today.'

We get up. Returning home in a rickshaw, Omar says, 'In our school, nobody, not even the principal, knows our real address. If anybody asks, we say our father works in an NGO.'

'We have been to the houses of our classmates,' says Omar. 'They are so different. In their homes, fathers work and children study. Women wear dupattas. In our house, women sit casually, with or without the dupatta.'

Osman says, 'In their houses, no one uses bad language.'

Omar says, 'In GB Road, women don't offer namaz. In their houses, people are always religious.'

After a few moments of quiet, Omar says, 'Sometimes I ask Abbu to leave this place and live somewhere else. But he says we won't get such a comfortable life elsewhere.'

The brothers don't have any friends in GB Road. 'Abbu doesn't let us go out,' says Omar.

'What happens to children growing up there?' I ask.

'They learn to speak bad words,' answers Omar. 'They wear unwashed clothes. They don't study. They become pimps.'

Osman says in a very man-of-the-world manner, 'If a girl is born in GB Road, the shadow of this place falls on her.'

Our rickshaw enters GB Road. 'When I'm big, I will leave this place,' says Osman.

'We will go to Noida,' says Omar determinedly, referring to a nearby township that embodies middle-class respectability.

SABIR BHAI IS WATCHING THE NEWS on TV. The screen flashes breaking news: 'Woman sub-inspector murdered by her husband and son'. 'Soofi, there is one thing that's been troubling me since the earthquake in Japan,' Sabir Bhai says, turning off the TV. 'Old

Delhi has been dug up to make way for metro rail lines. If there is a bomb blast underground, I'm worried our houses might fall down.'

'That's very unlikely.' Trying to sound casual, I query him, 'Sabir Bhai, you had an American man coming to your house?'

'You mean James? He was a nice man. Don't know where he disappeared. He had been coming for ten years. We would see him once a week or once in fifteen days or once a month. He'd always stay for at least two or three days.

'Yes, he loved us. Once, when the children were dressed in *sherwani* for Eid prayers, he was so moved looking at them that he started crying.

'He couldn't speak Hindi and I couldn't speak English so we communicated in sign language. Initially, he would go to that kotha,' Sabir Bhai says, pointing to the facing kotha whose entrance faces number 300. Its inhabitants have always looked at me with suspicion. 'Since James had so much money and he gave it so easily, the women there constantly exploited him. For instance, they charged him 500 rupees for a cigarette or for an ice cube in the beer. One curious thing about him was that though he did not mind paying, he would always kick the person after paying him or her. Nobody objected. Even the beat constables took money from him. They would laugh while being kicked by him. We did not like his insulting behaviour and asked him not to enter our house. I think that made an impression on him. He understood we were not after his money. So each time he entered that kotha, he would turn towards us and say, "Good, good. You good people." Finally, one day he entered our house. We never asked for his money and he never kicked us. But we never refused if he gave money to us.

'James never kept any change in his pocket. He always had this wad of 500-rupee notes from which he gave money to anyone who asked. Each time he was in our house, this veranda would be

125

filled with people and he gave each one a 500-rupee note along with a kick.

'He would come with his driver. I think he lived in a farmhouse in Chattarpur. The driver told us that he had many dogs.'

'When did you see him last?'

'Phalak was then pregnant. He had said that if she gave birth to a girl, he would gift her one lakh rupees. When Imran was born and Phalak told him on the phone that it was a boy, he congratulated her but did not come. After a few days, Omar called him, asking him to come and he said, "Very busy." When Omar called again a week later, a voice said that the number doesn't exist.'

Imran is sleeping on a mattress laid out on the veranda floor. He is the son James never came to see. Sabir Bhai looks at him with love and pride.

I want to hear about James from Phalak. Though she is kind and always offers me chai and food, she has built a thick wall around herself that I cannot breach.

Phalak smiles, laughs, makes jokes and sometimes shouts at her children, but that is the most extreme emotion I see in her. She calls herself an ex-sex worker and so is in quiet retirement. She spends the entire day washing dishes and clothes or cooking food. When she has no chores to do, she sits with Imran on the stairs, feeding him, or else gossiping with the women who stand there waiting for customers.

Nighat Khala, despite being active in the business, never sits on the stairs. She is standing on the balcony, looking down at the street. 'Khala, who is your favourite among the four boys?'

Nighat closes her eyes as if in deep thought, before smiling beatifically and saying, 'My Masoom. He is so quiet, absorbed in his own world.'

'Khala, do you think of having children of your own?'

'Who doesn't?' She looks sideways as if talking to the wall. 'But there'd be so many problems. In school, they will ask for the father's name. What would I say? No, I don't want children. At least not as long as I'm in GB Road.'

IT IS ABOUT HALF PAST FIVE in the evening. Omar, Osman and Masoom are in school. The kotha is quiet. A golden ray of sunlight comes in from the balcony, passes through the bedroom and falls on the veranda floor. Nighat is upstairs with a customer. Phalak has taken Imran to a doctor's clinic in Sitaram Bazaar. He has developed pus-filled sores on his legs. Sabir Bhai is reading a newspaper.

Sumaira enters carrying a cardboard carton of Nirodh condoms. She had gone out to get a free supply from an NGO office. She is tired and breathing fast. I can sense the rise and fall of her chest. She sits on the floor and stares down blankly. Suddenly there is the sound of footsteps running up the stairs. The sound increases in intensity, but Sabir Bhai continues with his newspaper and Sumaira does not look alarmed. Now the sound comes closer and now it explodes. The boys are home.

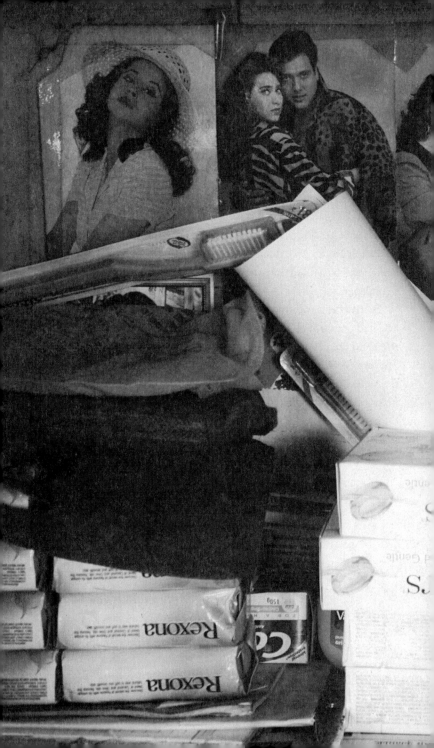

I love him the way
I loved him before

ONLY AFTER A FEW DAYS of not seeing her did I realize that Sushma was no longer in the kotha. I look for Omar. He is in the balcony with a small digital camera. 'Where is Sushma?' I ask.

'She said she was going to Meerut,' he says.

'When will she return?' I ask.

'Come on, Soofi,' says Omar, half his mind on the camera. 'People keep coming and going in this place. Even if they say that they are just going for a week, there is no guarantee you will see them again.'

'And where did you get this?' I ask, taking the camera from him. It fits in my palm.

'One uncle took us to Palika Bazaar.'

There is only one photograph in the camera. It is a blurred image of Omar, Osman, Masoom and Nighat. They are standing with a man, who seems to be in his thirties. He has a moustache. They are beaming. They seem to be in some cell-phone store.

'Who is he?' I ask.

Omar does not reply. He takes the camera back, asking me, 'Can you tell me how to delete this photo?'

I'M ON THE ROOF. Sushma's suitcase is nowhere to be seen. Her stove sits in one corner. The pressure cooker and a half-empty mustard-oil bottle are arranged against the wall. The bed is pushed towards the door. The mattress is lying neatly folded. The plastic basket holds a couple of onions. I walk to the balustrade and look down on the road. The traffic is flowing smoothly. On the railway tracks, a train with blue coaches is standing still. After a while, a rail engine blows its horn.

SHE IS NEW. 'Shh, nah,' says Nighat. We are on the veranda. I'm sitting with her on one bench and the new woman is on another. Dressed in a blue kurta and a brown salwar, she is looking towards the balcony. 'Roopa lived with us a couple of years ago,' Nighat says. 'She then went to another kotha and now she is back.'

The new woman has smooth dark skin. Her brown eyes are huge. Her hair has been patted down with so much oil that it sticks to her head like another layer of skin. It is parted in the middle by a delicate line. She wears no make-up, no necklace, no rings. There are burn marks on the left side of her chin. Talking softly, Nighat says, 'She is from Bihar. She had gone home to deliver a child but the baby died. So she is being very silent.'

A few minutes later, Sabir Bhai emerges from the latrine. Sitting down beside me, he says, 'Roopa is from Kolkata.'

I turn to her. She does not shift her gaze from the balcony. After a few moments, I look away, look down at the floor, and when I raise my eyes again, Roopa is looking at me. But she immediately turns her face away and covers her mouth with her hand. Is she smiling?

IT IS AFTERNOON. Roopa is eating dal and rice straight from a steel bowl. Her hands have the orange tint of henna. She is making little balls of rice and tossing them expertly into her mouth. I sit by her side. Roopa looks up and pushes the bowl towards me.

'Are you married?' she asks. I shake my head. She points to my prematurely greying hair.

'Are you?' I ask. She nods, tossing another ball into her mouth.

'I'M MARRIED,' Roopa says. We are sitting on the bench in the veranda. It is an early evening in summer. There is no electricity. 'He lives in the village. Near Kolkata. I got married about twenty years ago.'

'You look so young!'

'I'm thirty-five. I had a love marriage. He was Abbu's friend. Abbu was a rickshaw-puller in Kolkata and so was he. I lived with ammi in the village.'

Sherni, the dead rabbit's mate, comes running. Roopa raises her feet and rests them on the bench. 'We had a small farm. It was the size of this veranda. We grew cauliflower, brinjal and tomato. Once in fifteen days, depending on the harvest, Ammi and I would take the train to Kolkata—it would take about an hour and a half—and sell the vegetables on the Howrah Bridge. Abbu would also join us. At night, we would eat in a hotel and then sleep on the bridge.'

'So you met your husband in Kolkata?'

'Ravi Mandal. He was a Hindu but he converted to Islam, my religion. Once Abbu brought him to our village. He stayed for three or four days and I fell in love with him. He didn't have bad habits. He did not drink. He was like Abbu. He also earned quite well. When he started visiting us more often, he would give money and clothes to Ammi. We hardly had money to buy new clothes.

'I also liked his conversation. When I heard him talk, I felt this man was so nice. He would chat with all of us: Abbu, Ammi and me. He talked about farming, about crops, about household affairs. He always said that husbands must keep their wives happy and that a man should regularly give gifts to his woman.

133

'He was tall, about five and a half feet, and had a broad chest. His face was round and his complexion was very fair. He had a bushy moustache. He always wore white clothes. If you looked at him, you wouldn't realize that he was just a rickshaw-puller.

'Soofi, it's time for customers. I must get ready.'

'So, I TOLD MY ABBU, "Abbu, I want to marry him. I like him."' We are on the veranda. The children are at school. Phalak and Fatima are washing clothes in the bathroom. Imran is dragging a toy cycle. Sabir Bhai is sleeping. Nighat is sitting with us, listening to Roopa. 'Abbu said, "Let me ask him. If he agrees, I will have to find out where he is from and about his family."

'We never got to know about his parents. He had been living in Kolkata for two years. Anyway, it didn't matter. He agreed to the marriage. He told Abbu that he would live in the village for a year and only then would he marry me.'

'He wanted to live with you without marrying you?'

'It wasn't like that. We had two rooms. Abbu came with him to live in the village. They would both sleep in one room, and me and Ammi in the other.'

Nighat nods as if someone has just explained to her the solution to a complicated mathematical puzzle. As I look at her, she winks.

'We had a court marriage after a year,' Roopa continued, 'Our wedding papers are still with me. Then we started living together in one room. He started pulling a rickshaw in the village.'

'IN THIS LINE, a woman earns on her own. She doesn't really need a husband. Yet, she wants a man because she is afraid of men,' says Sabir Bhai. It is after midnight. The house is silent. Most people are asleep. Fatima is serving us dal and roti. Again, we are on the veranda. Nighat is sleeping on a mattress laid on the floor. 'Whether she lives in society or in a red light area, a woman needs

134

protection. Almost every woman in GB Road has her partner, whom she calls her *aadmi*, her man. This man is her protector. A woman can't survive without a man. If she hasn't got a man, men will tease her, molest her. They will try to grab her money.'

As Fatima gives us rotis and walks back to the kitchen, I wonder who her man is, or was. Sabir Bhai?

'Say, a woman is in her room and four or five customers enter,' says Sabir Bhai. 'If they start abusing her and beating her up, who will rescue her? If she has her man, he will come to protect her.'

After we wash our hands in the washbasin, Sabir Bhai says, 'Every woman wants a house, a husband and children.' Nighat turns in her bed, gently snoring. 'It is also practical for a woman to have a husband,' says Sabir Bhai. 'If she has small children, she can either take care of them or entertain the customer—she can't do both. If she chooses to be with her babies, how will she earn money? But if there is a man in the house, he'll look after the children while she looks after her customer.'

'I HAD TO PUT UP WITH a lot of hardship,' says Roopa. We are on the veranda. Nighat is listening to us with one ear, the other tuned to a film on TV. 'He took to the bottle a year after marriage. If I tried to stop him drinking, he would beat me up. Abbu had gone back to Kolkata, and in his absence, my husband would sometimes throw me and Ammi out of the house. We would stay in our uncle's house for two or three days and then return home.'

Pulling up her kurta's sleeve, Roopa shows me a dark circle on her left arm. 'Once my roti was not shaped round enough, he got so angry that he stabbed me with my rolling pin here . . .' she pointed to injury marks on her forehead, which I hadn't noticed before '. . . and here. I got five stitches in the hospital.' Roopa then turns around and lifts her kurta. I'm a bit embarrassed, until I see half a dozen burn marks on her back. 'After smoking a cigarette, he would burn my skin with the smouldering stub.' She pulls down the neckline of her kurta. There are six burn marks on her breasts. 'One day he was so angry that he grasped my right arm and twisted it around.

'He always came home drunk and would get upset if dinner wasn't ready. Finally, he sold his rickshaw and we lost all expectation of a steady income from him. Sometimes he would work on somebody's land for a day, but whatever money he earned was spent on alcohol. Sometimes he made a hundred rupees or so by carrying some farmer's vegetables to Kolkata. During one of Abbu's visits home, I stole 2700 rupees from his bag to get my husband a new rickshaw. The beatings stopped. But he sold this rickshaw, too, after three months. The beatings started again, and then he left for Kolkata for a year.

'We heard he once again had a rickshaw and that he slept in a rickshaw stand near the Howrah Bridge. Whenever Ammi and I visited Kolkata to see Abbu, we also met him. Sometimes he gave us money.'

A customer comes and Roopa gets up. She takes him to a cell behind the veranda, next to the kitchen. I'm left with Nighat. We can hear sounds from Roopa's room. 'Khala, have you ever fallen in love?' I ask Nighat.

'Never.'

Roopa emerges after fifteen minutes. She pats her customer's shoulders as he leaves, telling him soothingly, 'Come again.' She then washes her hands.

'He returned to us in the village, and stopped drinking,' Roopa says of her husband. 'Abbu arranged a rickshaw for him. He began to earn again. I was pregnant. But he started keeping bad company. He wouldn't come home for as long as two days. He spent the night sleeping on pavements. We would search for him and bring him home. Ammi would try to explain our situation. She would say, "Don't drink. Keep whatever you earn at home. Set up your own house, buy some land, tomorrow you will have children. How will you feed them?"'

Nighat is now staring at Roopa, her eyes wide.

'But he wouldn't understand. He would say, "No, I don't want a home. I want whisky." One night, he kicked me in the stomach. It was my seventh month. My child died.

'I was in great pain. Ammi and Abbu took me to the hospital. They paid all the expenses. My husband did not come to the hospital. My parents got me an operation so that I never have to bear a child again.'

I turn to Nighat. She had told me that Roopa had recently lost a baby during childbirth.

'The operation was necessary. Abbu said, "He drinks, he beats you, he doesn't give you food and clothes. If you have no children, at least you can go anywhere and earn for yourself."'

'Did they ask your permission before telling the doctor to operate on you?'

'I said, "Yes, do it."'

After a long pause, she says, 'I wanted to end my dependence on this man.'

SABIR BHAI HAS A BOIL in his groin. He is showing it to me.

'It has been hurting since yesterday. I have rubbed cream,' he says.

'Tell me Bhaijaan, how does a woman here marry? Is it a traditional ceremony?' I ask.

'They don't marry,' Sabir Bhai says, covering up his thighs with his checked lungi. 'This bazaar has a panchayat, an informal group of elders. Every one of us is connected to this group. When a woman and a man decide to live together, the panchayat gets to

know about it; from there the news spreads to others. When the couple separates, the news spreads in a similar way.'

'Do marriages break up often?'

'It is rare that the same man lasts for more than a year or two in a woman's life. But yes, I know some who remained couples till one of the partners died. A few marriages have lasted for decades and continue to survive.'

'I FIRST GOT TO KNOW about this line through a woman who lived in the village,' says Roopa. 'She took me to Sonagachi, the red light district in Kolkata. From there I came to GB Road. I've been here for five years. Or is it six? Let me count.'

We are on the rooftop. Once Sushma had cooked food for me here.

'Your mother knows you are in this line?' I ask.

'I came here to support Ammi. She has no one else to feed her. Abbu died of a heart attack. Ammi knows of my work. But when I visit her, she never talks about it. In this world, Soofi, no one becomes yours if you don't have money.

'My husband thinks I'm a servant in some household in Delhi. He now lives with Ammi. He is a changed man. He takes care of Ammi. He cooks for her. Once Ammi fell down and broke her leg. He took her to the hospital.'

'Will this be a permanent transformation?'

'I don't know. I don't understand him. But Ammi is not really happy. It is not about him. It hurts her that her daughter has to live so far away. I do what I can. Each month I send 2000 rupees to her by money order.'

Looking up at a crow soaring above our roof, Roopa says, 'I married of my own will. I liked him. I can't complain to anybody that he abused me.'

Suddenly, her voice filling up with passion, Roopa says, 'I will go anywhere, earn by any means, support my ammi and . . . also my husband.'

'Do you still love him?'

'I love him the way I loved him before.'

'You have never fallen for a customer?'

'God promise, I've never, ever loved anybody else. Look, I get three or four customers daily. While I'm with them, I only think that I have to earn money and send it home.'

Turning to me, she says, 'I often think of my husband. I talk to him regularly on the phone. I don't have a mobile. I go to the telephone booth. I tell him to take care of Ammi. I tell him that he should eat well and that he should make sure that Ammi also eats well. I ask him teasingly, "Do I sometimes appear in your dreams?"'

'He says, "Yaar, I cannot sleep. You must come soon."'

'I tell him that he must sleep with a pillow until I return.

'Sometimes he talks about the past. He confesses that he did wrong things. He asks for my forgiveness. He asks me to come back. I tell him that I will visit him and Ammi in a few months. I called him yesterday and he asked me to bring some ready-made pant–shirt for him from Delhi.'

'And you would get it for him?' I ask.

'What to do? He's my husband. He was very good to me in the early days of the marriage. He made *gajar halwa* for me. Since I couldn't make round rotis, he would roll out the dough for me. Sometimes he got mutton for me and cooked it himself. He was very fond of my *sewai* and biryani. Sometimes he asked me to massage his body. Sometimes he lay down on his back and I would walk over him.'

Feeling an urge for chai, I prepare to go down the stairs. Roopa follows. In the veranda, Nighat is holding Imran in her arms, patting him to sleep.

'Sometimes, I think . . . I think that if my husband hadn't strayed, I would not have been living in GB Road. But I'm here now. I'm making my own future.'

Struggling with her thoughts, Roopa says resolutely, as if she has decided on a plan, 'I will save money. When I'm old, I'll start a shop.

Okay, now I must get a customer.' While leaving me, she says, 'The grief set aside by the sod will always stay by your side. I think of him and I laugh. He was so stupid. He had such a good wife and he made her run away. He was so stupid.'

IT IS FRIDAY NOON. Sabir Bhai has gone with the children to Jama Masjid for prayers. Roopa is standing outside in the arcade with other women, soliciting customers. Phalak has gone to Sitaram Bazaar. Fatima is in the kitchen. Sumaira has gone to get idlis for Nighat's breakfast. Nighat is, as always, sitting on the veranda waiting for customers to come to her.

'How long have you been in GB Road?' I ask her.

'What difference does it make?' she says.

Among all the women in number 300, Nighat, or Khala, as the children call her, is the gentlest. I have never heard her raise her voice or utter a swear word. She is always dressed in clean salwar suits, and always wears a dupatta. She is the only woman in the kotha who does not eat paan, so she is the only one there who does not have her teeth stained permanently red.

Every time I enter the kotha, she gets up to make chai for me. Her voice is soft and she unfailingly asks about my mother's health each new day I meet her, although she knows nothing about my mother. When we talk, she sometimes rests her hand on my shoulders. Rather than being beautiful, Nighat has a homely charm to her, and I feel a kind of affection I might have felt for an elder cousin.

'Soofi, are you coming tomorrow?' Nighat asks.

'I think so. Why?'

'Can you get me a mobile-phone cover?' she takes out her Nokia cell phone to show me its size. 'It should be brown in colour.'

'No problem,' I say. 'I'll get it from Connaught Place.'

'You asked about . . . I've been here, I think, for fourteen years.'

'Where were you before?'

'Come on, where would I be? With my parents in Bangalore. You know, right, that Phalak is my sister?'

'You lived in Bangalore city or in some nearby village?'

'I've always lived in cities.'

'Did you have a boyfriend there, Khala?'

'What are you talking, Soofi! I have never had an affair with anyone. In Bangalore, I never did anything dirty that might have compromised my mother. Anyway, I was busy making bidis throughout the day.'

'You worked in a bidi factory?'

'No, we made bidis at home. All of us worked. Every day, from 9 in the morning till 8 in the evening, we would make about a thousand bidis. But we would get only nine rupees out of that hard work.

'Papa died of cancer a few years after Indira Gandhi was killed. He was a carpenter. We were seven sisters and one brother. Phalak was the eldest. I was in between. After Papa went away, we had a difficult time. Ma was ready to wash dishes in other people's houses but we couldn't let her work as long as we were alive. Our young brother was going to school and we had to pay for his education, too. But he did not like studies and decided to apprentice himself to a tailor. We married off five sisters while Phalak and I entered this line.

'First Phalak came here. Fatima didi . . . she is also from Bangalore . . . she brought Phalak here. After four or five years, I came.'

'Your mother didn't object?'

'Initially, she didn't know. Gradually, she got an idea of our line but what could she have done? Our father was no more. We had no elder brother. Who would have looked after us?'

Roopa comes up and enters the veranda with a customer. She takes him to her cell behind the veranda.

'Soofi, what do you know about what happens when there is nothing to eat at home,' Nighat says.

Roopa reappears after a minute. She is singing an old chartbuster from a Hindi film. '*Karte hain hum pyar Mr India se . . .*' She gives Rs 150 to Khala, who touches it to her forehead. This is the day's first earning.

'What kind of boy did you want to marry as a young girl in Bangalore?' I ask.

Nighat does not have to think before answering. 'Shah Rukh Khan. I first saw him in *Baazigar*. I saw the film in the picture hall with the entire family. In the film, Shah Rukh's father is very rich during Shah Rukh's childhood but their property is taken from them by the villain. When Shah Rukh grows up, he takes revenge on that man by duping his daughters into falling in love with him.'

'I have seen the film. Shah Rukh kills one of the daughters.'

'He has to take his revenge. I liked the way Shah Rukh portrayed his helplessness and anger at the way this world works. Most people are cheats.'

'But Shah Rukh Khan is a fantasy. What sort of a real-world man did you want for a husband?'

'Somebody just like Shah Rukh. I would have been happy if I'd got someone who had a job, who did not drink, and who was not into beating his wife. I dreamed of a man who would remain faithful to me till the end and who would never doubt my character.'

'You have been in GB Road for fourteen years. You've never liked any customer?'

'Customers are selfish. Once their work is done, they are like, "Who are you and who am I?" We can't trust these men. Sometimes a man might visit us regularly but the moment he sees a prettier girl, he would immediately dump you for her. So what can you do? Nothing!'

Omar's camera had a picture of Nighat with the children and a man in a Palika Bazaar store. Was he a customer?

'In all these years, I did like one customer,' she says. 'He was a regular but he has stopped coming. The poor man must have a wife and children. What could he do? I liked his attitude. He never acted like a customer. He always greeted you like an old friend. Most customers are useless people. They come drunk, speak bad language and ask you to do it like this or that. But I tell such people, "No brother, take your money and go back."

'But this man was different. He was like a family member. He would chat with the children. We would talk for hours. He asked me why I entered this line. Once he said that I should have lived a married life. I replied that a woman needs to have a large dowry to find a husband. I explained to him that this line is not that bad. We would talk for hours like a real husband and wife.

'I'm not sure if I miss him but one does remember good people. He must be happy with his family.'

'Did you want to marry him?'

'Why would anyone with a wife and children have anything to do with me? They have a reputation to keep in society.

'There are times when I think of the possibility of marriage. Everyone wants to marry, but I don't like this system. Don't you hear about so-and-so girl getting married after her parents have paid a large dowry and even then the husband is no good? He leaves the girl. But yes, if the girl is born lucky, she'll marry and live happily till the day of her death.'

'Sabir Bhai told me that every woman in GB Road has a man.'

'Most women have pimps as their so-called husbands but I'll never hitch myself to a man while living in GB Road. What's the point? Live for two days with one man, then leave him and pick another . . . in this dirty line, you get disgraced even more. The fact is that I'm alone and I'll remain alone.'

Roopa comes in with another man. He seems to be on a high and is walking in a daze. Nighat says, 'Careful.' At the other end of the veranda, Fatima is combing her hair in front of the mirror.

'I have met many customers who say they want to marry me,' Nighat says. 'But I don't fall for such promises. I know what happens next. He'll take me into society, and start abusing me for being a woman without character after four days of living together. Then I would be thrown out of his house and I'd have to come back to GB Road.'

'Do you ever feel lonely?'

'I'm used to it. Loneliness does not have everything to do with GB Road. I have been feeling it since I was a child. But when I think about my life . . . if my future is better than my present, I may get a husband.'

We can hear a thumping sound from Roopa's cell.

'Roopa is getting many customers today,' I say.

'Ch,' says Nighat. 'She goes downstairs to pick customers. I will never do it. I don't like to stand on the road.'

Soon, Roopa comes out of her room. She is scolding the customer in a tone of mock annoyance. 'Why are you saying that I am like your wife? Will you marry me? Tell me?' The customer looks love-struck. 'Why are you staring at me?' Turning to us, she says, 'Mother's cunt! He was calling me his sister while fucking me.'

145

The customer is adjusting his trousers. Roopa forces him out of the veranda. She then turns to ask me, 'Soofi, should I get you Pepsi?' Just then another man comes and Roopa takes him to her room.

'Look at Roopa,' Nighat says. 'She married her man. He beat her up. Now she is in GB Road. Why marry then?'

After making me chai, Nighat says, 'Fifteen years ago, my uncle's son wanted to marry me. He was an engineer in Bangalore. If I had married him, he would have looked after me, not my family.'

We finish our tea in silence.

'Now he is married with two children,' Nighat says.

'Do you regret refusing him?'

'If I'm doing this dirty work, it is for my people—my sisters, my brother, my mother. Ma has a sugar problem. She needs a lot of money every month for medicine. Bhai is a tailor and earns well only during the festive season. My sisters got married. Their husbands look after them and their children.'

Roopa enters with two men and signals to Nighat, who gets up and takes the older man to her room upstairs. Roopa takes the younger man to hers. I'm left with Fatima, who is still combing her hair. 'Sometimes Roopa picks up customers for Nighat,' she says, coming towards the bench where I'm sitting. Roopa shouts from the room, saying earnestly, 'Nighat is from a good family. She cannot go downstairs.'

FATIMA IS IN HER SIXTIES. When she stands by the balcony and the sun's rays fall on her brown eyes, she looks beautiful. Like Sushma, she stays awake at night. She no longer entertains customers but solicits them for Sushma and other women in teen sau. Like Roopa, she was already married when she arrived in GB Road. Unlike Roopa, her husband never abused her.

147

'I was married at twelve. We lived in Bangalore. My father was a hakim. My mother cooked at home. But they died in my childhood and my elder sister married me to a bidi worker. Syed Mehboob was twenty-two. He had no parents. He made bidis at home and earned a few rupees every day. It was like "earn today, eat today, with nothing for tomorrow". He died at thirty-five. Somebody did black magic on him. He fell down and injured his leg. There was a swelling in it and after a few days he died. I had four boys and one girl from him. The boys are now married and Munni, my girl, lives with one of them.'

Talking of her husband, Fatima says, 'He gave me no trouble. He used to sing qawwalis in the dargah. I would sit in one corner of the courtyard and listen to him. He could sing all the songs of Muhammed Rafi. We were left with no money after his death. I came to GB Road. Munni was then three months old. I left the boys at my sister's place. I came to Sabir's establishment.'

'How long ago was this?'

'It's been now more than twenty-five years. In this life, there's no contentment.'

'Why do you say that?'

'I have never been able to have another person in my life. If a customer became regular and too fond of a woman, Sabir would bar him from the kotha. He was afraid I would run away. I was very pretty when I was young. Sometimes, foreign customers who had visited me would write me letters from their homes in Saudi Arabia and Pakistan, but Sabir would return the letters with a note, saying that I had left the place. You know, so far five girls have run away from Sabir's kotha with their customers. Phalak and I got trapped.'

Phalak looks so satisfied managing her children, who call Sabir their Abbu and of whom Sabir is so fond, that I could not imagine her being trapped.

148

'Sabir didn't succeed in life. And he didn't let us succeed either,' says Fatima.

'Among all the regular customers you had during different times, is there anyone you remember with special regard?' I ask.

After thinking for a minute, Fatima says, 'There was Shamim, about twenty years ago. He was a Muslim and he would talk about religion to me. He told me that I should pray five times daily and that I should keep fasts during Ramzan. After four years of visiting me regularly, he said he wanted to marry me.

'I refused. I had children. He stopped coming. I saw him after a few years. He said, "You refused. So I married another woman."'

SUSHMA IS BACK from Meerut. She is on the roof with a man who seems to be younger than her. They are both slicing tomatoes. Sushma looks up at me with annoyance. 'I don't have free time. Go downstairs.'

The veranda has a guest. Much fuss is being made over him. 'He was a regular customer,' Fatima says. 'We are seeing him after three years. He had gone to Dubai.'

The man is in brown trousers and a blue T-shirt. He has a paunch. He looks embarrassed by the attention.

'Eh, why have you become so black?' Fatima asks him.

'And so fat too,' Nighat says. Her hands are on the man's thighs. She asks, 'Married?'

The man blushes and shakes his head.

'How come you became so fat in Dubai?' Fatima asks. 'I have heard that they have no spices in their food. Even then you ate so much?'

Nighat says, 'You must have been eating a lot of chicken and biryani.'

The man finally speaks. 'I cooked at home.'

'Take me to Connaught Place or Karol Bagh,' Nighat says, laughing. 'I won't shop for anything above a thousand rupees.'

Roopa comes out from her cell with a seemingly satisfied customer. Sitting down on the bench, she asks the foreign-returned man, 'Come on, you must treat us to beer. You must have made lakhs in Dubai.'

Nighat says, 'You must go back to Dubai. If you stay in Delhi, you will do nothing and keep coming to GB Road.' They all laugh.

Fatima whispers something into the man's ear and takes him inside, to Roopa's room. They stay there for a long time. Roopa goes down in search of customers.

'Is he an old customer of Fatima's?' I ask Nighat.

'He is an old customer of all of us,' she says.

'Then why is he sitting inside alone with Fatima?'

'He will sit with each of us. Fatima took him inside to ask for money.'

'Will he give her some?'

Nighat laughs. 'No way, he never gives anything.'

'WHY DID YOU SNUB ME yesterday?' I ask Sushma. She is washing her clothes on the roof.

'I was with a friend. We were planning to drink beer. I did not want you to watch me drinking.'

'Who was that man?'

'He is very close to me.'

I feel betrayed. I have had intimate talks with Sushma on this roof, and while she has shared stories of her life with me, she never told me about this special man.

'What does he do?'

Sushma gets up, walks to the balustrade and lights a bidi. 'I like him but I don't know for how long he will like me.'

A religious procession is moving slowly on the road. A few young men are holding a giant statue of goddess Durga on their shoulders. A cry goes up '*Jai mata di!*' Looking down at them, Sushma says, 'He is a mechanic in Meerut. He will come as long as she is interested in me.' Durga is bobbing up and down in a sea of men. 'Men keep coming and going. When they leave us, we cannot go after them.'

O God, please
send us customers

IT IS DUSK. The young priest is getting ready to invoke the gods. Two women, seemingly in their late twenties, step in. Wearing salwar kameez, they appear freshly bathed, their dark, smooth skin glowing, long hair streaming down their shoulders.

Pracheen Hanuman Mandir is the only temple in GB Road. It is a two-minute walk from number 300. The temple has idols of various gods and goddesses, including Durga and Kali. It also has four cows. I go to the priest and whisper, 'Panditji, who are these two women? Have they come from upstairs?' In GB Road, 'upstairs' is the code word for kothas. The priest, lighting an earthen lamp, replies, 'Everyone who comes here is a child of God.'

The temple is on the right-hand side of the road, separated from the tarmac by a tiled platform. Traffic moves slowly down the road. Many passers-by stop in front of the temple, send up a silent prayer with a quick dip of the head and walk away. A few take off their shoes and enter. One man comes in carrying a box of sweets. He hands it to the priest, who keeps the box at the feet of Hanuman's statue for a moment before returning it to the man. The sweets are now blessed. The man leaves after respectfully placing Rs 10 on a ceremonial steel platter. The two women have sat down on the temple floor. An elderly Sikh man in a safari

153

suit enters. Without interrupting his mobile phone conversation, he rings the temple bell, puts a tenner on the platter and leaves.

The evening traffic has slowed to the speed of sludge, the impatient honking from various vehicles butting into the spiritual quest of the temple devotees. The women look very familiar. They are definitely from somewhere upstairs. I have seen them on the balcony of some kotha, wearing bras and petticoats, calling out to the men below. But here, they look so different. Could I be mistaken? One of them takes off her dupatta. After bundling her hair into a knot, she drapes her dupatta to cover her head.

The priest picks up the brass bell and starts ringing it with his left hand. His other hand holds the steel platter, which he moves in a circular motion before the figure of Hanuman. The women get up. One starts clapping; the other begins to ring a bell that hangs from the ceiling. Two men walk in from the road and they too start ringing the temple bells. The air is filled with a deafening clamour. The ears throb. After a minute, the shock subsides, the sound finds a rhythm and my ears adjust to it. The clapper is now tapping her fingertips against each other, in time with the ringing of the bells. The other is ringing the bell, faster and faster. More people join us. The priest is reciting a mantra, but nothing is audible except the syllable 'Om', which is repeated every few seconds.

Somebody starts blowing a conch shell, a deep, long boom growing in volume. The combined reverberations of the bells and the conch shell drown out every other sound. The traffic on the road has thickened further, but I can no longer hear the horns nor the cries of rickshaw-pullers. The priest is stopping in front of each idol, ringing the bell, offering the platter up to the deity. The woman ringing the bell has a pained expression on her face, as if she is grieving. The other resumes clapping with renewed vigour. Even in the sultry weather, her face is free of sweat beads. More

154

men have come in. More bells are rung. It feels as if the vibrations produced by the bells are clearing the air of GB Road of all its smoke and smells. The woman ringing the bell is beginning to perspire, but her expression remains calm. Ringing the bell faster than before, her hand is moving in a blur.

The priest is now crying loudly. '*Har Har Mahadev!*'

The worshippers repeat after him. The bells swing faster.

'*Jai Hanumanji ki.*'

The worshippers echo that. The ringing becomes more urgent. Suddenly, the ringing stops. The aarti is over. The gong lingers.

WHILE SHOWING ME THE BOOK, Omar warns, 'Soofi, be very careful. Your feet should not touch it at all.' The book is in Urdu.

Explaining its sacredness, Osman says, 'It's about our Prophet.' We are sitting in the room next to the balcony. It is noon. Nighat is on the veranda, waiting for customers. Roopa is standing downstairs, calling out to men. Sabir Bhai is sleeping in his room.

'Allah created Shaitan out of fire,' Omar tells me, flipping through the book. 'And Allah made Adam out of clay and blew spirit into him—'

Osman interrupts, saying, 'The men grew out of Adam.'

Signalling him to hush up, Omar continues with his story: 'Allah ordered Shaitan to bow before Adam, but Shaitan refused to obey Allah. He now tries to seduce people into leaving the good path for the bad.'

I ask Omar, 'What is the bad path?' The boy is prompt with his response, 'To walk the dirty way, not to perform the namaz, not to keep fasts during Ramzan. This is Shaitan's doing. Suppose you have to go to Nizamuddin Dargah this evening, but as the hour when you have to leave the house approaches, Shaitan starts whispering into your ears, "Why go today? It's so hot and you won't get an auto easily. Why don't you go tomorrow evening?"'

Clasping my hand, Osman says, 'But if you do go to the dargah, you stay safe from Shaitan's influence. He cannot enter it.'

Omar adds, 'Yes, he can only climb the tree outside the dargah but can go no further.'

I take the book from Omar and start to turn its pages. Osman whispers into my ears, saying, 'There is a Shaitan under the earth. His name is Kana Dajjal. On the Day of Judgement, he will tell us to make him our Allah. Those of us who get scared of him will agree to his demand. Those who don't will go to the real God.' Omar stands up and goes out into the balcony.

Osman continues. 'There is a heavenly crown in the sky. After we are dead, only those who understood the Quran, explained its meaning to others and lived an honest life get to wear the crown.'

I go outside into the balcony. Omar is looking down at the pimps. There is a tin shed below the balcony. A black cat is sleeping there. Omar says, 'Soofi, sometimes women throw away their veils. That is wrong, too. In Islam, women should always be in burka.'

SABIR BHAI WILL NOT TOUCH any woman for the thirty days of Ramzan. During this holy month the believer has to remain clean, both physically and spiritually. He wakes up early in the morning for *sehri*, the pre-dawn meal, after which the fasting, *roza*, starts. Then he goes without food and water till sunset, the iftar hour, when he breaks the fast with fruit and dried dates. It is forbidden to have bad thoughts, or have sex during the hours of fasting, or touch anything unclean. Ideally, the women in Sabir Bhai's establishment too should stay away from the business, but customers cannot be turned away and money has to be earned. On the veranda, however, Nighat is careful not to sit beside Sabir Bhai. If he accidentally touches a woman who is taking in clients, Sabir Bhai immediately has to have a bath.

Fatima is slicing apples for iftar. The only woman in the kotha who is keeping the fast, she does not sit outside during the night this month. Today the feast will be somewhat lavish. I'm going out with Osman to get pakoras and a one-litre bottle of Coke. Sabir Bhai has given us a hundred-rupee note. While walking, Osman continues his Judgement Day story: 'Everyone will die. We will all be standing in one row. On one side, there will be Shaitan; on the other, Allah. Shaitan will be killed and Allah will examine each of us, determining our good and bad deeds.'

'How will he do that?' I ask.

'Soofi, do you know that every person has one angel sitting on each shoulder?' asks Osman. 'If you do bad things, the angel on your left shoulder makes a note of it. The good deeds are recorded by the angel on your right shoulder.' After a pause, he says, 'I fear for my mother.'

Stopping our discussion, we buy the pakoras and the Coke and return home, barely exchanging a word.

The prayers are about to start at Jama Masjid. Each of us is in a white salwar kurta. Sabir Bhai got one made for me by a tailor in Farash Khana. We have washed our ears, neck and arms in the ablution tank at the centre of the mosque courtyard. Because of the great crowd, the resident pigeons have temporarily left the courtyard and are sitting on the mosque's domes. Every Friday, Sabir Bhai comes here with the boys for the special afternoon prayers. Today, the children have returned early from school. This is the first time I'm with them in the mosque. Our blonde Imran is the centre of attraction with his lighter skin, white dress and cap, and blue velvet jacket. People are taking his picture on their mobile phones. Sabir Bhai mumbles proudly, 'He looks like a foreigner.'

THE FAST HAS JUST ENDED. After eating a few grapes, Sabir Bhai and Fatima have sat down to perform the namaz. This is a special prayer and it will last about half an hour. Omar and I are having halwa on the balcony. We are eating with our hands from the same bowl. Making a ball of halwa in his palm before popping it into his mouth, Omar says, 'Soofi, if we talk of the women here, there is no doubt that what they are doing is bad. Allah will examine them, too, on the Day of Judgement. And I know what he would say.'

Omar waits till he swallows the halwa. Then, raising his head, he closes his eyes and says, as if reciting a well-remembered poem, 'I forgive you. You are a poor woman. You must have had some compulsion. You had to fill the empty stomachs of your hungry babies.' Then opening his eyes and turning to me, Omar says, 'Allah will pardon her sins, and send her to heaven.'

Sabir Bhai is praying in his room, standing, bending, sitting down on the floor, kneeling, standing up again. 'You know, Soofi,' Omar says, 'Every Muslim is destined for heaven. But if you have sinned, you will be sent to hell.' Osman joins us with another bowl of halwa. 'Those who use swear words . . . Allah will put glowing coals on their tongue.' Pointing to the courtyard, Omar says, 'All customers who come here will go to hell. Shaitan is making them do sinful acts.'

'The food we are eating here has come from the money paid by these customers,' I say.

Osman snaps back, 'But it is our helplessness that is making us eat food from that money.'

Raising his arm as if to shut up his younger brother, Omar says, 'Soofi, you know there are mullahs who have read the entire Quran . . . they are called hafiz. But some of these people don't share their knowledge with poor children. One such mullah stopped teaching us the Quran because Abbu could not pay him regularly.' Osman says, 'Yes, Mehboob master, who was supposed to teach us God's words, will go to hell.'

HE TAPS ME ON MY SHOULDER from behind. I jump. Mehboob is matchstick-thin, his cheeks hollow, his eyes sunken; his beard is light brown and scraggly. He is in a white salwar kurta and wears a white skullcap. He cannot be older than twenty-five. I got his cell-phone number from Sabir Bhai. We arranged to meet outside a fruit juice parlour, next to Turkman Gate.

Mehboob leads me to his room. We turn right into a narrow lane crowded with goats. I'd been waiting in the sun for half an hour and now my T-shirt was sticking to my back. As we walk ahead, the lane gets narrower. The jutting balconies of the houses facing each other nearly touch, blocking out the sky, creating some shade.

The cleric turns into a door on the right. The temperature inside is several degrees higher—it is like entering an oven. 'There is a printing factory here,' Mehboob says, walking up the stairs. 'It is cooler in my room above.' The wooden stairs are creaky. There are no electric bulbs. Mehboob's room is on the second landing. A gust of cool air greets us as we enter. The cooler is running. The walls are painted green. The small room has a single cot, a bookshelf and an old-fashioned desktop computer. One wall has a large vinyl poster of the Swiss countryside. A bearded man in checked lungi and white vest is lying on the bed. He gets up as we walk in. 'Naseem is my roommate,' Mehboob says.

The room has no windows. The shelf has only Urdu books. Mehboob hands me a bottle of Sprite and a pack of potato chips. He says nothing more, though, as he sits there looking shy. This, my host, is the one destined for hell, according to Sabir Bhai's sons. 'Why did you stop teaching them the Quran?' I ask.

Mehboob bows his head, looks at the floor for a few moments, turns to Naseem, smiles and then again gazes at the floor. He looks embarrassed.

I take a sip of Sprite. 'How did you find them? Did you first visit their kotha?'

Immediately covering his ears with his hands, as if he cannot let such bad words go through his eardrums, Mehboob says, 'No, no, no. I was training to be a maulana and somebody told me that a kotha owner in GB Road was looking for someone to teach the Quran to his children. So, I went there. I would otherwise have never gone to that area. It is haram. I thought that maybe I could be a good influence on the children of prostitutes.'

Waving at his room-mate, Naseem says, 'Mehboob is very religious. Initially, he was very uncomfortable at the thought of going to GB Road every evening. What if somebody saw him there and reported it to his family in Bihar? His parents would not understand.'

'But I gathered my courage,' says Mehboob. 'I thought that Allah had directed me to teach the Quran to those children. If they could understand the concepts of the Book, perhaps they would try to get out of that world.

'I taught them for almost a year. Then I got a part-time job in an Urdu newspaper where I had to work evenings. So it was no longer possible for me to go to the kotha.

'In Islam, it is not good for Muslims to do what they are doing. But how can I judge them? They are helpless. The Quran is divine. It has no author and it has everything that you need to understand Islam. It clearly says that having sex with someone who is not your spouse is haram. On the Day of Judgement, the people who have disobeyed Allah will go to hell.'

I'm thinking of the women I know in teen sau number. 'Will Nighat also go to hell?' I ask.

After thinking for half a minute, Mehboob shrugs and says, 'That is Allah's will.'

'What about Sabir Bhai?' I ask.

'If he fasts during Ramzan,' says Mehboob, 'if he prays five times daily, if he goes to Jama Masjid every Friday, he will get his due. At the same time, if you are doing bad things, you will be punished . . .'

Naseem interrupts, saying, 'Just praying, fasting and believing in Allah is not enough. Islam is a religion where you have to follow each command of God. You cannot do what Allah has forbidden. You have to perform only those things that Allah has asked you to do. In Islam, some doors are closed, and some are open.'

Mehboob says, 'Allah has created this universe to serve men. We have to surrender to his will. If we act against his wishes, we will obviously be punished.'

The power goes off. The room has no window and it is now dark. Naseem says, 'The root of evil in that kotha is Sabir. He is making the women do that business. He is the one who is living off that money. How does it matter if he goes to Jama Masjid every week?'

The room is getting hotter. Fanning himself with a newspaper, Mehboob says, 'I never charged a fee from Sabir. I only took the conveyance money.'

Drenched in sweat, I get up to leave. Seeing me out to the street, Mehboob says, 'Once I asked Phalak why she entered this trade, and she said she had problems at home. But so many people have problems at home and outside too. Does it mean they should all join this line?'

THE SKY IS LOSING ITS BLUE. The temple bells have started ringing in Pracheen Hanuman Mandir. Fatima is preparing herself for the evening ritual. She has bathed, and now she picks up the

163

matchbox and enters Sabir Bhai's room. She lights incense sticks for the framed portrait of the Kalyar Sharif Sufi shrine and for the calendar images of Mecca, and of Lakshmi, Ganesha and Saraswati that hang on the wall. On the veranda, incense sticks are lighted for the framed photograph of Hazrat Nizamuddin's Sufi shrine that hangs above the bench where the women sit while waiting for customers. Then it is the turn of Jesus Christ, Shiva, Krishna and Guru Nanak. Finally, Fatima goes to the entrance door and lights a stick for the framed calligraphy of Kalima, the Muslim declaration of faith: 'There is no god but God. Muhammad is His messenger.'

The entire kotha has been perfumed.

'You are a Mussulman, so why did you bow your head to Lakshmi?' I ask Fatima. 'God is one,' she says. 'Incense sticks are put up everywhere, whether it is a temple or a dargah.' Taking some water from a bottle in her hand, she sprinkles a few drops on the door, the veranda floor and me. 'This water has come from the Hanuman Mandir downstairs. It is sacred.'

Handing me a cup of chai, Phalak says, 'Lakshmi is the goddess of wealth and this house is a *dukaan* (shop). We have to keep Lakshmi happy and make her feel wanted.'

Roopa comes up with a customer. He wants to know the time. She points to her salwar and says with a laugh, 'Do you think this is your mother's watch?'

Sitting on the bench, Fatima says resignedly, shaking her head, 'Why did God send us here?'

Nighat comes down with a customer. She gently pats him on his shoulder and asks him to come again. Sitting beside me, she crosses her legs and looks at the TV as if she is watching a soap opera, though the set is switched off.

'All my life, I have done dirty work. But now I keep fasts so that God can direct me to heaven,' Fatima says.

Taking Nighat's hand and running my finger on a line on her palm, I ask, 'Why don't you fast during Ramzan, Khala?'

She frowns in mock anger and exclaims, 'Why should I? I will do that when I reach Fatima's age.'

Since Roopa's cell is just behind the veranda, next to the kitchen, we can hear her as she loudly scolds her customer. 'I'll hit you if you do that,' she says. 'Motherfucker, raise the leg again. Yes, like that.'

Looking at me, Fatima says, 'Soofi, eat some apples. You are so thin. Build your body. Marry and have children. Who knows how long you will live? Leave behind your offspring, before you die.'

Roopa comes out with her customer. She nods at me, smiling shyly, and goes down in search of customers.

Phalak gets up and fetches half a dozen brinjals from the kitchen. Sitting down on the floor, she starts dicing them. Roopa reappears with a new man. 'Sister's cunt!' she says, loudly. 'He's a bloody rickshaw–wallah.' Fatima laughs. Soon, we hear Roopa crying, 'God, you smell real bad. My heart is sinking.'

Nighat shakes her head, saying, 'Delhi men are filthy. They don't bathe.' Phalak says, 'When I was working, I would only take clean customers.'

'What if he stank?' I ask.

'I would politely ask him to leave,' she says.

'Brother, please spare me,' Nighat exclaims, her face contorting into a damsel-in-distress expression. We laugh.

IT IS A WARM EVENING. The crowd has gathered to celebrate the *urs* or death anniversary of the Sufi saint Hazrat Nizamuddin Auliya in his dargah. The dome is lit up with electric bulbs. The courtyard is packed. After the prayers, there will be qawwalis lasting for the entire night. Special food stalls have been set up around the lanes leading to the shrine. Some pilgrims are wearing

pointy yellow caps. Yellow was Hazrat Nizamuddin's favourite colour. Families linger around the dargah's several graves. The punkah–wallahs are fanning the pilgrims. One of them has only one arm. Suddenly, I hear a familiar voice: 'Soofi.' It is Omar. Behind him are Osman and Masoom. Imran is in Sabir Bhai's arms. Someone puts a hand on my shoulder. It is Fatima. We stay together for the rest of the night.

SHOPS ARE ROLLING DOWN their shutters. The lights are coming on. Phalak is feeding gular leaves to the rabbit and the children are playing on the terrace. Fatima is sprinkling temple water over the courtyard. Downstairs in the arcade, the air smells of dust, smoke and sewage. Roopa is leaning against a pillar, dressed in a plain purple nightie and, for modesty's sake, a dupatta. This is unusual for somebody whom I have always seen dressed in flashier clothes, like velvet salwar suits.

'What happened? Why the nightie?' I ask.

'I'm not well, Soofi. I have stomach ache and fever.'

'Take some rest, then.'

'Motherfucker Sabir won't let me. I was sleeping but he asked me to come down.'

Embarrassed by this unflattering reference to a man whom I consider my friend, I turn the conversation. 'Roopa, do you ever pray?'

'Soofi, I do it daily during Ramzan. All thirty days. Otherwise, I pray only on Friday.'

'Why not daily?'

'I cannot. I have to get clients, too. And when my body is dirty, how can I perform namaz?'

A young man approaches Roopa. She gives him her arm, and they go upstairs. By now, the bells have started ringing in Hanuman Mandir. A few women from number 248 come down and stand outside the entrance of their kotha, forming a half-circle. The oldest among them has a broom in her right arm and she moves it seven times in a circular motion. After completing each circle, she says, 'O God, please send us customers this evening. O God, please send us customers. O God, please send us customers . . .'

It will be an hour before the evening prayers start. I will have enough time to talk to him. Pandit Hans Raj Sharma has small living quarters in the temple precincts. He has long curly hair, a wavy beard and very smooth skin.

Pracheen Hanuman Mandir is also known as *pyau*, a place where one gets free drinking water. It is also called *gaushala* because of its cowshed. 'The temple was set up by my grandfather, who came from Rajasthan,' says Sharma. 'After him, my father took care of it. Now, the heritage has been passed to me.' The water used to be drawn out of a bore well, till the GB Road Market Association installed two water coolers in the temple. Anybody can come and drink the water.

Opposite the temple, across the road, is a boundary wall that separates GB Road from the railway shunting yard. A message is painted on the wall:

CONDOM EK
SURAKSHA ANEK
(One condom
Many protections)

The temple shed has four cows. Like the gods, they get offerings, too. People from Dal Market to Ajmeri Gate come to offer them rotis. 'What about women from the kothas? Do they come too?' I ask.

'People come from various places—from the back-lanes and, yes, from upstairs, too,' Sharma says. 'We cannot stop anyone from entering temples or mosques.

'When these women come to pray, they take a bath and put on clean clothes. They talk in low whispers and call me brother. They don't behave the way they do when they are standing in the arcade or on their balconies.

'Sometimes they have problems and they ask me for solutions. Only this morning, a woman came from upstairs and requested help. She said that the price of food items has gone up and that her earnings are not enough. She wasn't getting customers. I asked her to feed cows with spinach, chana dal, jaggery and rotis. If you are kind to animals, you get peace of mind.'

Getting up to bathe the idols, Sharma says, 'Most women end up in this place because of their own mistakes. Sometimes they are cheated; sometimes they have to leave their homes. And once a woman starts making her living here, she cannot go back to her family. If she goes back, she won't get respect.'

'Panditji, the Muslim women I know in GB Road sometimes pray to Hindu gods.'

'Yes, many of them come here to pray. Some Muslim women call me to their kothas to perform Satyanarayan puja. In GB Road, many women follow both faiths. It is about their souls.'

THE DARGAH OF Imam Ullah Shah *urf* Laddu Shah Baba is the only Sufi shrine in GB Road. It comprises a small chamber. The walls are inlaid with white tiles, and so is the tomb. A few tiles are painted with flowers. Flies buzz on the floor.

The shrine is built around the trunk of a neem tree, which grows above the dargah's roof into a towering network of leafy branches. The chamber has two arched entrances. The one with a striped curtain is the principal doorway. The other is locked with an iron gate, outside which grows a sadabahar tree. Its leaves enter through the gate's square openings and peep into Laddu Shah's tomb.

A door set in the chamber's side wall opens into a larger room. This is the family room of the dargah's caretaker, Muhammed Ikram. He runs a tea stall next to the shrine. The family has four women: Ikram's mother, his sister, wife and daughter. The biggest piece of furniture in their room is a sewing machine. 'We sew our own clothes,' says Rukkayya Begum, the mother, before asking, 'Are you a Hindu?' Nadira, the sister, says, 'Hindus also come to pray at the dargah.' She points to a slab outside that says the tiles were laid by Mool Chand Sharma, a trader from Punjab, in gratitude for the fulfilment of his wishes. Pointing to a dusty chandelier hanging from the domed ceiling, she says that a Hindu shopkeeper had installed it.

The women have no idea about Laddu Shah's life. I go to Ikram, who is at the tea stall. 'My father knew about the Baba,' he says. But the father died a decade ago, and lies buried in a graveyard near Dilli Gate.

The dargah celebrates the urs of its saint, every year in mid-August. A goat is sacrificed, and for three days, qawwalis are performed and khichdi is served free to visitors.

Unlike most Sufi shrines, Laddu Shah's dargah is only partially serene. The sounds of the traffic and the cries of vendors never quite recede. A worshipper sitting on the dargah floor can see the outside world as a stream of cars, motorbikes and rickshaws. Across the road, in kotha number 467, sex workers stand on their second-floor balconies.

'Do these women visit the shrine?' I ask Rukkayya Begum. 'Yes, they come,' she says. 'They offer flowers, drop a few coins in the donation box, pray and leave. We don't talk to them.'

Every day I bring customers to the kotha

BEWARE OF

PICKPOCKETS AND PIMPS

This is the warning painted on the wall along every staircase leading to every GB Road kotha.

IT IS DARK. The sky is overcast, the heat sweltering. The street lights have given up, all but one. The shops are shut, and even the traffic has taken leave of GB Road. The only sound is of a Hindi film song playing somewhere. Across the road, there is some sign of life: two men urinate against the wall.

'Where are they?' I ask Omar.

'You should have come last night. The corridor was milling with them,' Omar says. We are in the balcony. It is midnight.

'Look, rickshaw!' Omar whispers. 'You see those two guys running after it? See that boy in the blue T-shirt? They are pimps.'

The rickshaw is speeding along the empty road, carrying a lone passenger. The rickshaw-puller starts pedalling faster, as the boys chase it.

'Now, they will climb the rickshaw, take out their knife and rob the man . . . wallet, watch and mobile,' Omar says.

Not tonight. The rickshaw is too fast for them; the boys turn back. The road is empty again.

IT HAS JUST STOPPED RAINING. Roopa is in the arcade, looking agitated. Another woman—waiting for customers—is buying karela from a vegetable vendor. Suddenly, Roopa lets out a yell, 'You daughter of a slut.' I cannot figure out to whom it is directed. I climb the stairs.

Nighat is sitting on the veranda in a see-through black maxi. This is the first time I'm seeing her in a Western outfit. She sits with her legs crossed, palms resting on her lap. Her hair is combed into a thick bun. In the room that opens to the balcony, Sushma is sitting on the floor, alongside Sabir Bhai, who is sewing a pouch of green silk. A piece of paper is folded inside the cloth. Sushma, too, is sewing a similar pouch. Because of the heat, she has lifted her kurta, exposing her midriff. She is wearing glasses. As she leans forward, the neckline drops, revealing her breasts.

'This is *taveez* for the boys,' says Sabir Bhai. 'Verses from the Quran have been jotted down on these bits of paper. When the children wear it round their neck, they will no longer have nightmares.'

Phalak enters and declares that she is off to Chandni Chowk. Sabir Bhai affectionately addresses her as Lambi, the tall one. Phalak laughs and call him Charsi. 'Why is she calling you Charsi?' I ask.

'Because I used to smoke charas a great deal,' Sabir Bhai says.

'Here, people get names,' says Sushma, her eyes focused on the needle. 'If you are seen drinking *sharaab* (wine), you are *sharaabi*. If you are seen smoking smack, you are smackey.'

Suddenly, Sabir Bhai stops sewing, raises his head, looks at the wall facing him, and asks no one in particular, 'How to get rid of my nickname?'

I too have a question. 'I understand that we should be careful of pickpockets. But why of pimps? Don't they help in getting customers?' I ask Sabir Bhai.

'They rob customers, who stop coming after that. And if they don't come, where would we be?' he says, putting down the needle. He stretches out his legs, adjusts his lungi, and continues, 'Pimps were always there in GB Road, but until ten years ago, they were not a menace. In fact, in the old times, you would never see a woman downstairs in the kotha. It was not considered respectable. The women stayed inside the kotha. The pimps were stationed outside on the road and got customers for the women they worked for. They operated on a commission basis. So, if a pimp brought a customer to the woman, she would give him twenty per cent of her fee. If the customer was happy with the pimp's services, he might give him extra money.'

'Things were simpler,' says Sushma. 'The pimp brought the man to the woman and he was not a nuisance.'

Sabir Bhai adds, 'About one per cent of the women here had their own husbands working as pimps.' Masoom is sitting beside me, listening to us.

'Pimps had standards,' recalls Sushma. 'They wore clean clothes and they never swore. They were rarely aggressive or pushy with customers.'

'A decade ago, a new set of pimps came in, must be about a hundred,' says Sabir Bhai. 'They were criminals and were on the run from their hometowns. They had no morals, no stakes in the business and no inhibitions about robbing customers. Old women who had great difficulty getting customers tied up with them. These pimps would tell unsuspecting men that they were being taken to young, fair girls from Nepal and Kashmir. Then, when a customer came face-to-face with an old woman, he obviously turned away, but wouldn't be allowed to leave until he parted with his cash and valuables.'

Sushma picks up the thread of the story. 'Gradually, word spread that people are robbed in GB Road. And we lost many regular clients because they were afraid to enter the area.'

'The pimps are protected by the customers' own sense of embarrassment. It is rare for a robbed customer to go to the police,' says Sabir Bhai. 'Most men come here discreetly and they don't want anyone—definitely not the cops—to know that they were visiting a prostitute. But you know something? Those customers who do file an FIR almost always get their money back.'

'And the pimp is promptly arrested and put behind bars,' Sushma adds.

'There is an understanding with the police. The pimp is always charged with some small offence. His kotha madam provides the bail and he is back on the street within days,' confides Sabir Bhai.

'The pimp might not be universally liked,' I say, 'but it is ironic he is in the pay of the same kothas that ask customers to be alert to pimps.'

'But these are only a few kothas,' Sabir Bhai says. 'Honest sex workers have suffered because of these pimps.'

An AUTORICKSHAW IS SLOWLY making its way through the afternoon traffic. It stops and is immediately surrounded by a ring of pimps. I witness the scene from the balcony, where I am seated having chai with Sabir Bhai. A man emerges from the rickshaw. He can be seen gesticulating at the pimps. The driver also steps out . . . and then gets back into the auto immediately. One of the pimps grabs the man's arm. He turns pale. The other pimps start laughing. Suddenly, the man wrenches his arm free and jumps into the vehicle. The driver starts the auto, and as it begins moving, one of the pimps manages to clamber in.

'See,' Sabir Bhai says, 'This man was not even a customer. He was just passing through and those bastards are bothering him. Soon no one will come here. The pimps are destroying GB Road.'

'YOU ARE A KASHMIRI so you need to be doubly caref—' Sabir Bhai breaks off in mid-sentence as I enter the veranda. A slim unshaven man is standing near the washbasin. His hands are behind his back, and his head is lowered. He is smiling sheepishly, like a child getting a gentle scolding from his mother. Roopa is standing in the gallery that leads to the latrine. She looks embarrassed. There is an abrupt silence as I enter, as if I have invaded a family's private moment.

'So, Abdul, don't do this. If the police get you, you will be in real trouble,' Sabir Bhai says. 'I won't be able to help you out. You don't have any ID card. Even I don't know anything about you. You are from Kashmir. Who knows, you might be a terrorist.' Roopa walks out to the veranda, and before she can say anything, Sabir Bhai says, 'Of course, you are not. But who will explain that to the police?'

Roopa laughs nervously and takes the Kashmiri's arm and drags him outside.

'Who is he?' I ask. Sabir Bhai says, 'He is a nobody.' I persist. Sabir Bhai replies, 'He was a labourer who used to come from Kashmir in the winter. But now, instead of pulling trolleys from Ajmeri Gate to Khari Baoli, he pimps for number 288.'

'What was he doing here?'

'Something is cooking between him and Roopa.'

I go out. Roopa and the Kashmiri are sitting on the stairs, holding hands and talking in whispers. Her head is on his shoulder. I turn back, leaving them alone.

MAMTA IS THE NEWEST ADDITION to number 300. She is a tiny woman in her early twenties, reaching only up to my shoulders.

She is so thin that her clothes hang on her like an ironed shirt on a hanger. Her skin is almost black and her eyes are chocolate brown. During the day she hangs around in the arcade, calling out to men. She is extremely friendly. When she spots me coming, she hurriedly walks towards me, takes my arm and escorts me to the stairs as if personally responsible for my security.

Sometimes, we both spend the afternoon on the rooftop. I read my novel-of-the-day and she stands by the parapet, looking down at the road. Occasionally, she comes over to me and affectionately ruffles my hair. She always looks happy, as if she is content with her life.

It is early evening and I'm standing with Mamta in the arcade, keeping my distance from her so that potential customers don't shy away. An old man walks past. Mamta taps him on his shoulder, saying, 'Yes, darling, I'm waiting for you. Come now.' The man looks at her with irritation, adjusts his shirt and walks away. Another man walks past. Mamta starts singing a Hindi film song from the eighties.

> Yeh ladka mere saamne
> Mera dil liye jaye
> (A boy in front of me
> Is taking my heart away)

This man pays no attention. Two young men go past. Mamta shouts, 'Oye, your money!' The boys turn and Mamta laughs at her own joke.

Another man approaches. Mamta stops laughing. The man's well-built body seems to be bursting out of his tight long-sleeved shirt and trousers. He looks angrily at Mamta. She returns the look. 'You bloody pimp,' she says.

STATION KAMLA MARKE
NTRAL DISTT DELHI

क्या आपने मुझे कहीं देखा है ?

SHO. P.S. K. Mk
INSP. PARMOD JOS

Div. Officer:- S.I. AJAY SIN
Asst. Div. Officer:- ASI. PURAN CHA

BEAT   H.C. VIJENDER
OFFICER:- H.C. BALJEET SIN
           H.C. BALARAM

ASST. Beat   CT. SANDEEP
OFFICER:-   CT. YOGESH
             CT. KANWAL KIS
             CT. BIJENDER
             CT. RAJKUMA
             CT. CHHATRPA
             W/CT. SUSHMA
             W/CT. SARITA

कृप्या मेरी मदद कीजिए 100 नं० व

थाना कमला मार्केट फोन नं०- 23230623, 23233743
पर इन्तला दीजिए   धन्यवाद

The man walks closer and says, 'Whore, I will get you picked up one of these days.'

'I will dig out your eyes,' Mamta retorts.

'Bitch, you would dare touch me?'

'Bastard! Was your father a pimp, too? Did he fuck his own mother?'

As they exchange barbs, the rest of the women laugh. The man, too, is smiling. The only one genuinely agitated is Mamta. Roopa, standing near the pillars, tells me that this pimp was Mamta's lover when she lived in another kotha. He left her after she became pregnant.

'Where is her child?'

'I don't know,' says Roopa.

I repeat the question upstairs, to Nighat.

'I've heard that she went to Bombay when she was about to deliver,' Nighat says. 'She returned only a week ago.'

'What happened to her child?'

'I don't know,' Khala says. 'And why should I bother? Soofi, let me warn you, Mamta often uses our lipstick and nail polish without telling us. Beware of her.'

WHEN I WAS NEW to GB Road, the pimps would always follow me, promising women from different provinces. They made me so nervous that I would avoid even eye contact with them. Sometimes, a particularly aggressive pimp would tap on my shoulder or grab my arm, not to rob me but to make me go with him. Hiding my fear, I would keep walking straight, faster.

Soon, I devised a strategy. I did what I do while walking down a street teeming with stray dogs. The dogs might growl and bark, and sometimes follow me, but I walk past them as if I were the king of the street and the dogs didn't exist. The animals would then never bother me. That trick always worked. And it worked in GB Road too. Within a few months, the pimps stopped harassing me.

Perhaps a regular to the red light district shows certain characteristics: an air of determination to him, looking like he knows where he is going, not casting curious glances at the kothas upstairs. The pimps know where he is headed and realize that it is pointless to meddle with him.

THE BOY IS STANDING beside a water trolley, next to the entrance to the railway shunting yard, across the road from a kotha. He is perhaps twenty years old, and has soft facial hair; his mustard-green checked shirt is unbuttoned to his waist. Our eyes briefly meet.

'So, you are a *dalal*?' I say, using the Hindi word for pimp.

He nods. I ask, 'What is your name?'

'Why should I tell you?' he says. As I start walking away, he calls out to me, 'I know you. You go to number 300 daily.' He says 'I know you' in English.

'Where did you learn to speak English so fluently?' I ask. He laughs, playfully unzips his denim trousers, zips up and says, 'I do pimping because I have problems in life.'

The boy is a portrait in accessories: two earrings on the same earlobe, a pendant and a bracelet. There is a tattoo on each arm: a bleeding heart, and a girl's face with a rose between her lips.

'Your girlfriend?' I ask, pointing to the tattoo.

'I've never had sex,' he says, again unzipping his jeans. He is staring at my crotch.

'Where is your family?'

'They live in Gonda,' he says, referring to a faraway town.

'Do they know what . . . '

'I've told them that I drive an autorickshaw.'

'Isn't that a job you could have done?'

'I started by being a dishwasher in a dhaba. Afterwards, I drove an auto . . .'

'Then why did you take to pimping?'

'As I said, there were problems . . . my father has a farm in the village . . . it's small . . . but we grow rice and wheat. Anyway, now I pimp for 288 and I get a salary of 6000 rupees each month from the kotha madam. I send half of it to my parents.'

'Whose face is on your pendant?'

He turns the locket around and shows the portrait of Sai Baba.

'Please don't take it personally,' I say, 'but every door on every kotha is painted with the warning that customers should beware of pimps. Do you sometimes rob people?'

'It is just the phobia of these women,' he says, rolling his eyes. 'Every day, I take customers to the kotha and I never misbehave with them. Don't believe in everything you are told here.'

'Where do you sleep?' I ask.

'I've taken a room on rent in Lakshmi Nagar,' he says. 'I share it with two other boys.'

'Are they also pimps?'

'No, one is doing a coaching course for the engineering entrance exam. The other works in a mobile phone showroom. They know I'm a pimp.'

'Have you ever got them women?'

'Never. We are decent people and don't indulge in these things,' he waves his arm, taking in the entire length of GB Road. He asks me, 'Are you hungry? I always have my lunch in the dhaba. A plate of karhi–chawal for 15 rupees.'

'I'm in a hurry.'

'Ever since I was a child, I've wanted to do something in life. I want the world to notice me. I don't mean I want to make a big name in the underworld, but I want to achieve something by doing good work.'

The boy's Nokia cell phone rings. I catch fragments of the conversation. 'Haan . . . make some food . . . dal and roti is fine . . . but don't forget to get my clothes ironed . . . I'll start in another half hour.'

'Sometimes, when somebody wants to be especially vicious to another man, he abuses him by calling him *dalla*, which is slang for dalal,' I say. 'And you are actually a dalla. So, suppose I walk past you and call you dalla, what will you do?'

The young man says, 'First, I will ask you very politely, "Don't you have manners? Is this what your parents taught you?" If you again call me a dalla, I'll say, "This is my work." And if you repeat it for the third time, I won't say anything. I'll just slap you.'

'Soofi, have some ice cream. Please.' I'm with Mamta in the arcade. She is waiting for customers. An ice-cream man is walking down the road with his cart. Roopa is talking to a woman from another kotha. Mamta's attention shifts from the ice-cream man to a rabri–wallah approaching us. Dressed in a white dhoti–kurta, he balances a steel bucket on his head. As he puts it down, Roopa peers into it and says, 'Have you masturbated into it?' Mamta makes a face and says, 'Chee! Who knows if this man has washed his hands or not?' The man ladles out the rabri in a leaf bowl. Suddenly, Mamta points to a boy leaning against a pillar on our right and says, 'Soofi, he is a dalla.'

The pimp looks like he is barely out of his teens. His yellow T-shirt has a slogan printed in red:

BEING SEXY IS A CRIME

As I walk towards him, I hear Mamta shouting to someone, 'Will you give me money, darling?'

The boy's eyes are red. He smells of whisky. Just as I open my mouth to talk to him, a voice says, 'No, sisterfucker. Don't say a word. Go away.' This aggressive outburst comes from a woman sitting in a rickshaw. She is in a cream-coloured salwar suit, with a black dupatta covering her head. Until a moment ago, I'd not clocked her presence; she was part of the landscape of people making up the traffic. Had I noticed her earlier, she would have seemed to me a housewife from Farash Khana who would never set foot in GB Road unless she had to cross it on her way to the station.

But the rickshaw is stationary and the woman is possibly a madam, and the pimp must be on her payroll. She had addressed her words to him. Turning to me, the madam joins her hands in a namaste. With cold politeness, she says in English, 'Please. No talk with my dalal.'

MASOOM IS WATCHING *POKEMON* on the cartoon channel. Sabir Bhai is cutting a news item from the city page of the *Hindustan Times*. I can see the headline: 'Sex racket busted, Sonu Punjaban's kin held'. Osman is talking to me in soft whispers. 'Some pimps are younger than me,' he says. 'Yesterday, I'd walked over to Shahganj to get jalebis. Returning, I had just stepped into the corridor, when I saw a boy following a customer. He was saying, "Come, I'll take you to 251. It has Nepalis, Assamese, Bengalis."'

'Who could this boy be?' I ask.

'I saw him for the first time. Mostly, these boys end up here after running away from home.'

THE PIMP IS LYING SPREADEAGLED in the corridor, blocking the way. He is unconscious. His grey cotton trousers are wet, perhaps with his urine. I jump over him. 'It is the doing of their employers,' says Sabir Bhai. It is late evening and I'm returning home. Sabir Bhai is accompanying me till Ajmeri Gate. 'The madams always happen to be old. They no longer receive customers but still need a man for themselves. So, they hire these boys as pimps; the boys also satisfy the madams' need for sex.'

I ask, 'Why would these boys want to have sex with them when there are so many young women here?'

'That's why these madams turn them into smack addicts,' Sabir Bhai says. 'The boys are then completely dependent on them and are ready to do anything as long as they get their fix.'

I'M FOLLOWING THE PIMP. We cross number 300, go past the temple, and as Farash Khana comes up around the corner, he turns and asks me, 'Have I done anything to you?'

'No,' I say. 'I only want to know how you get into this business.' He stares suspiciously. I try to explain. 'I'm writing about this place and most of the women I know here say that pimps are bad people. But you look like you wouldn't even hurt a fly.'

The young man is wearing a yellow shirt with grey shorts and yellow leather sandals. His eyes dart around, resting on something behind me. I turn around and spot two constables walking in our direction. 'Look, I'll talk to you,' the pimp says, 'But the cops are coming. Let's pretend that you are asking for directions to Khari Baoli.'

The constables look carefully at us but don't stop. 'I'm Rajiv Sharma, and I'm twenty-three; I'm from Himachal Pradesh,' the pimp says. 'Should I tell you about my family?'

I nod.

'My parents are in the village. My brother is in Jaipur. I've told my parents that I work in a tea shop in Jodhpur. So when I call them from my mobile phone, I use a Rajasthan SIM card.'

Another pimp walks over to us and listens. Rajiv scowls at him. The other pimp responds with an insult, 'You bloody sister's penis.'

'Do you have a woman?' I ask.

'I had one. I married her. She worked here. We had a court marriage. She now lives in society. We have a one-room house in Sector 22, Rohini. She no longer does the wrong sort of work.'

Walking back towards the temple, Rajiv says, 'I came to this place five years ago. I used to come here to enjoy myself. I liked it so much that I started coming regularly. Soon, I started living here. I left my job in a dhaba where I used to peel vegetables. The madam in number 362 hired me.'

'You met your wife in that kotha?'

'No. You can't enjoy yourself in the kotha where you work. When you start living in a kotha, the people there become your family. How can you enjoy yourself with your mothers and sisters? So I would go to other kothas. Met my wife in 354.'

As we reach number 300, Rajiv says, 'No one thinks much of Sabir's women. You must go to 362. It has fair women from Nepal, Kashmir, Assam and Bengal. It is also very safe and comfortable. The rooms are air-conditioned. If you want, I can take you there. Pick any woman of your choice.'

THE EVENING AARTI is reaching its climax in the temple. The sky is a bluish black. The rooftop is in darkness. Sushma is frying meat pieces on the stove; its blue flames are leaping about the karahi. Mamta is standing at the parapet, her hand under her chin. I'm lying on the floor, on Sushma's mattress. We can hear the whistle of a railway engine.

These women. They are so open, yet so closed. Their bodies are commodities, available to anybody who can pay. Their life stories, especially when they focus on why they became sex workers, are almost identical. But there is something in each woman that makes her distinct. There is no person like Sushma in the world, and I am frustrated by my inability to grasp the essence of her personality. She shares her feelings with me but only to an extent and only on occasion. It is the same with Roopa, Nighat and Mamta. They guard their thoughts and memories more closely than others. Could it be they cherish the secrecy because there is no secrecy about their bodies?

Mamta is quiet. Is she watching the traffic or the trains in the shunting yard? Is she thinking about the pimp who made her pregnant? Is she missing her child, if he or she was even born?

I open my shoulder bag and take out the talisman I always keep with me when I come to GB Road. These five stapled pages are a short story by the Urdu writer Saadat Hasan Manto. I'd got this English translation photocopied from a friend's book. *The Black Salwar* is set in Delhi in the 1940s and is about a sex worker. There is no mention of GB Road, but the landmarks and the buildings described by the author place the story firmly in this area.

Mamta is looking towards the railway yard, from where train engines whistle at irregular intervals. I turn to the third page of the story. Under the glow of my cell-phone torch, I reread one of my favourite passages:

> Railway engines and carriages went by constantly, in one direction or the other: there was a perpetual noise of moving trains. If Sultana came out on [the] balcony early in the morning, she could see thick clouds of smoke emerging from the vents of the engines, clouds that rose slowly, like fat and heavy men, towards the murky sky. From the rails seemed to issue rolling bundles of steam that quickly evaporated into the air. Whenever she saw a carriage that had been propelled by an engine and then left to advance on its own, Sultana was reminded of her life. Like that lone carriage, she had been propelled on the tracks of life and then abandoned; other people were changing tracks, but she continued to move in the same direction. Where she

187

was headed for, she did not know. And then, one day, she would lose the impetus that had moved her and she would stop somewhere, at a place of which she knew nothing.

Manto's story centres on a prostitute called Sultana who has just moved to Delhi's red light district from a town in Punjab. Not getting enough customers, she is left with little money and concentrates all her energies on getting a new black salwar that she can wear during Muharram. The story has two male characters. Shankar, the man who gets Sultana her black salwar, appears in the middle of the story. He is clever and flirtatious. He regularly walks in the red light area, looking up at the prostitutes standing on the balconies. He is so charming that the women might even have sex with him for free. Khudha Baksh, the other man, is the more important person in Sultana's life—he is the pimp who convinces her to move to Delhi—but Manto forgets him as soon as he summons Shankar into the story.

When I read *The Black Salwar* for the first time, the sexual chemistry between Shankar and Sultana eclipsed Khuda Baksh. But, on repeated readings, Baksh's character grew on me. In a few pages, Manto had depicted a life that conveyed the substance of a pimp's character, without passing any judgement. Baksh is a lorry driver who convinces a Kashmiri girl to run away with him. He turns her into a prostitute and lives off her earnings. After a few years, when the girl runs away with her lover, Baksh goes to another town in search of her, and there he finds Sultana, who has already established herself as a sex worker. They like each other and start living together.

After Baksh sets himself up as a portrait photographer, his clients—mainly British soldiers—become Sultana's customers. Life unravels when Baksh convinces her to move to Delhi's red light district. In the big city, Sultana's business doesn't pick up. Men rarely come to her and those who come pay her far less than what she used to get. Sultana has to sell her gold bangles. Meanwhile, Khuda Baksh visits a fakir, hoping he will help turn their luck. It is at this point that Shankar enters and Khuda Baksh disappears.

The brevity of Khudha Baksh's story is appropriate. Although he had been in Sultana's life for longer, her moments with Shankar—she meets him just three times—are more lasting and deep.

Early in the story, Sultana decides to live with Khuda Baksh not because she loves him but because she considers him lucky for her business. As a pimp, Baksh influences the external circumstances of her life, but he has no power over her inner self. Perhaps this is the pimp's ultimate destiny. Other than bringing customers to women, he doesn't matter much. His role is brief. Perhaps Mamta is thinking of someone else, and not the pimp who made her pregnant.

For decent people
like us

ONE CATEGORY OF MEN whom the sex workers never bother is the shopkeepers downstairs. It is odd to watch these traders carry on with their business of sanitary fittings, sitting under the garlanded black-and-white portraits of their ancestors while just above their showrooms, the world's oldest business is transacted every day.

Does the thought of what is happening upstairs cross their mind?

Most shopkeepers refused to talk. Finally, one agrees. Dressed in a muddy-brown coat and trousers, and speaking English in a British accent, he declines to give his name and declines to talk about the women. Instead, he starts discoursing on, of all things, Pearl S. Buck's novel *The Good Earth*.

'It shows the true spirit of Asia,' he says, 'as well as the pathetic lives of our peasants and how much worse their condition becomes when they have to leave their villages for our great cities.'

My attempt to steer the talk to the GB Road kothas offends him.

'Shopkeepers are the most honourable people in our society and we have never touched these women, never talked to them. The women, too, never come to our shops.'

Maybe he is right. The women in number 300 talk of freely moving around the city—Sitaram Bazaar, Connaught Place, Mehrauli, Nizamuddin Dargah and, also, Golcha cinema in Daryaganj—but do not mention the shops downstairs.

'Most men who come to or pass through GB Road instinctively look up to watch us but never the shopkeepers,' Nighat had told me. 'We too never make a pass at them.'

The shopkeepers and the sex workers manage to coexist by pretending that the other does not exist.

ONE AFTERNOON I see three little schoolchildren, heavy bags bending their backs, walking hand in hand. An elderly shopkeeper beckons them and gives them orange toffees. The children giggle, take the surprise gift, say 'thank you', giggle again and walk up a stretch of the arcade before turning right and disappearing into an unlit staircase—upstairs, to a kotha, to what must be their home.

IN THE AFTERNOON RUSH, the traffic moves sluggishly. Some shops are busy with customers. Others are empty, save the owners and employees. I step inside one.

'Namaste,' I say.

The owner, sitting behind an aluminium table top, nods.

'Sir, I'm doing a book on GB Road, focusing on the lives of women who live upstairs, and I wanted to ask . . .'

'What do we have to do with them?' he says, cutting me off before I can finish the sentence.

'Actually, sir,' I speak fast to pre-empt another interruption, 'I want to understand exactly this: the women live above these shops and yet they are so removed from the world downstairs. How is that possible?'

'Look, this is business hour,' the shopkeeper says with annoyance, as if I'm a salesman trying to trick him into buying sub-standard products.

I ENTER THE STORE of Prakash & Sons. The man behind the wooden desk must be in his late thirties. He wears grey-rimmed glasses loosely perched on his nose. A blue towel is placed on his black leather-padded rotating chair. He greets me with a kind, welcoming smile. I introduce myself. He gestures me towards a chair across the table.

Most of the floor space in the shop is taken up by toilet seats, bath tubs and water faucets. The walls are layered with light-pink tiles. There are four landline phones on the man's desk. The shop is air-conditioned. On the wall, a framed portrait of goddess Durga wears a garland of marigold. The glass door of the shop faces a branch of the ICICI Bank across the street. A stream of pedestrians is passing by.

'This shop was started by my grandfather,' says Karun Abro. 'He had come from Lahore after the Partition. Usually, my father sits here. We have a showroom in Najafgarh, too,' he says, referring to a locality on the western fringes of Delhi, miles away from GB Road.

'So, you are writing a book about the women here,' he says. 'Earlier, they used to conduct their business in Chawri Bazaar.'

I ask him, 'Do you know anything about the women here?' Perhaps it was not the best way to frame such a delicate question. The man smiles, and says, 'In this market, every shopkeeper is busy with his work. You are so involved in the business that you don't know what's happening in the next shop. With the women upstairs . . . no, there is no interaction.'

'But surely there must be some occasion when you get to see those women? Maybe during some festival . . . maybe they come downstairs to greet you, or maybe there is some tradition . . .'

'What exactly is your book about?' he asks.

'It is on the various aspects of their lives. I have been spending time with them in a particular kotha. Now, I'm trying to understand how these women navigate the world outside the boundaries of their lives. I'm intrigued that while they live in such close proximity to shops like yours, they spend an entire lifetime without entering one.

'I also want to know if the fact that they live in this place affects—in any way—the lives of people who live and work in or around here but who are not part of their business. Let's say, a person like you.'

Karun Abro takes out the fountain pen from his shirt pocket, and rolling it across the desk, he asks, 'In its entirety, what is your book aiming to tell about these women?'

I take a deep breath. 'I'm perhaps trying to capture the ordinariness of their extraordinary lives. Their world has nothing in common with the one I live in. Yet, when I'm with them, everything . . . I mean everything, the fact that they swear in front of their children, that they have sex with strangers, that they live in such wretchedness, and that while perhaps this is not a life worth living, some of them are still so independent . . . I want to get a sense of all of this. I don't know if I can, but ideally I want this book to go into the heart of this uncivilized world . . . '

'What did you say?' He looks up. 'There is nothing uncivilized here.'

I'm surprised at my own choice of words. Is that how I think of the place I'm writing about?

Karun Abro is still playing with his pen.

'Go to any part of the world, and you'll find them. GB Road is a part of our society. How can you say that they are not civilized?

'There are a lot of things that you must have discovered about the women's lives upstairs—how they came here and so on—but you will skip some aspects and highlight others. And this manipulation will shape the image you present to your readers. You have the pen, you have the power.

194

'I might tell you fifty things about the women but you will write only about thirty things. I wish you well for your book, but it will never be an accurate portrait of your subjects.'

Ordering his assistant to bring chai for me, he starts talking again, 'Every shop here has a separate electric meter. The ladies upstairs get their own bill every month. We never meet. No shopkeeper interacts with them. No greetings are exchanged during any festival.'

FASIL ROAD IS THE NAME by which the elderly people in the area call the back lane that runs behind the shops and kothas, from Ajmeri Gate to Lahori Gate. It runs parallel to GB Road and separates it from other localities of Shahjahanabad.

'Fasil' means 'divider' in Persian. In the Mughal period, the royal capital was surrounded by a stone wall that guarded the city from the wilderness outside. Fasil was the border, the limits of the city. The pleasure women of Shahjahanabad had originally established themselves in Chawri Bazaar, where the red light area flourished until the British rule. After the women were moved from Chawri Bazaar to GB Road, the city's red light district acquired an address that reflects the dilemma of its position in society. Today, GB Road is just across the fasil, the original boundary of Shahjahanabad. The women who live here are of the city but not in it.

'IN OUR SOCIETY OF HYPOCRITES, we need those women and we also disown them,' says Hasan Khurshid, a 'legal journalist' who lives in a 150-year-old mansion in Farash Khana, a crowded bazaar of barber shops, bakeries and tea houses.

I'm sitting in Hasan Bhai's living room. We are a five-minute walk from GB Road, yet this is a different country. Hasan Bhai's house—it has a large courtyard, the walls of which are strung with bougainvillea creepers—is in Chatta Nawab Sahab, a quiet street lined with houses and mosques that have carved wooden doors set in arched entrances. The din of the bazaar does not reach us.

'In the old times, nawabs lived in this street,' Hasan Bhai says. 'The rest of the neighbourhood was filled with craftsmen and labourers who worked on carpeting the floors of palaces and pavilions in Red Fort; they also worked on the floors of the mansions of the rich in the city. The Urdu for floor is *farsh* and so the place began to be called Farash Khana, the place where farsh workers lived.'

Hasan Bhai speaks in flawless Urdu; his voice is low and his manners extremely polite. He addresses his four children with the respectful *aap*, instead of the informal *tum*. A Shia Muslim, his living room has a large portrait of Imam Husayn's mausoleum in Karbala. A devotee of Western classical music, his cell phone's ringtone is set to the climactic movement of Beethoven's Ninth Symphony. Before he enrolled for English honours at Zakir Hussain College, he was a student in the Anglo-Arabic College in Ajmeri Gate. Every day he walked to school. Every day he had to cross GB Road.

'It was somewhere in our subconscious that good people don't live there. Our parents told us that while walking on GB Road, we were not to look up. Now I'm fifty-six and I still don't look up. When I'm in a rickshaw going towards the metro station, I deliberately keep my eyes cast downwards. Sometimes I might want to see a bird or look at a hoarding, but I don't. There is a fear. If somebody known to my family catches me with my eyes raised, what would he think of me? For decent people like us, looking up at the kothas is taboo.'

Hasan Bhai's wife is in the kitchen making mutton korma for us. I see a koel in the guava tree in the courtyard.

'I cannot say I'm a poet, but sometimes I compose Urdu couplets in my mind and if I like what they convey, then I note them down

in my diary.' Rising from the sofa, he says, 'Once I had written a verse on the women who live in places like GB Road. Let me show it to you.' He goes to a battered wooden chest and shuffles through the files and books.

After a few minutes' search, he says, 'I don't remember where I kept it. But I remember a few lines. I had given it the title *Tawaif Kaun*, meaning "Who is a courtesan?" May I please share it with you?'

'Yes, please,' I say.

Yeh woh aurat hai
Tumhari nazar mein
Jiska jism sirf auratnuma hai
(This is that woman
Who in your eyes
Is a woman only because of her body)

Jise tumne kabhi aurat na maana
Magar darasal
Asli aurat yahi hai
(She is the one you never considered a woman
But in truth
She is the real woman)

Ye sabra-na-jabt ki hain putli
Tawaif isko tum kehte ho
Tum isko besawa keh lo
Ye sab kuch maan leti hain
Palat kar kuch nahin kehti
(She is the image of tolerance
You might call her a courtesan
Or you might call her a whore

She submits to all you say
She never talks back to you)

Yeh shafaf darpan hain
Har chand aaina hain
(She is like a mirror
As transparent and as pure)

MAMTA IS IN A GREY VELVET GOWN. A red dupatta is flung around her shoulders. As I set foot on the stairs, she greets me in English, saying, 'Soofi, hi. Welcome.' We shake hands. Her palm is rough and sweaty. Did she wash her hands after the last customer, I wonder.

Nighat is sleeping in the veranda, lying sprawled on the bench. Sushma is on the floor. Sabir Bhai is in his room, quietly smoking a cigarette. I sit down on a bench. The door to the balcony is closed but sunlight filters through the slits and falls in bands on the floor.

Two customers come in, look at me, look at Nighat and Sushma. One of them says, 'Whores, still sleeping.' They go down. A minute later, Mamta comes up with a man. Smiling at me, she takes the man to the cell adjacent to the kitchen. I'm sitting in the corner that looks sideways at the cell. A minute later, Mamta comes out, a 500-rupee note in her hand. She goes to Sabir Bhai's room to give the money to him. I quickly glance at the man in Mamta's room. He is in light-brown briefs and a white vest, and is tapping on his cell phone. Mamta returns. Three minutes later, she comes out again. The man is now zipping up his trousers. He rushes out, following Mamta. 'Give me my change,' he says. Mamta makes a face. 'What change? I don't have change,' Nighat and Sushma get up.

The man says, 'You told me downstairs it's a hundred rupees.'

199

'I don't have change,' Mamta says, washing her hands in the basin.

The man holds her by her shoulder. Mamta turns and pushes him towards me. I get up. Sabir Bhai comes out. 'Take this,' he says, giving three 100-rupee notes to the man. 'What would she do with just a hundred rupees? Forgive her. Give her 200 rupees at least. She must have quoted that sum to bring you up.'

The man takes the money from Sabir Bhai. Walking out of the door, he says, '500 is nothing for me but I can't be cheated.'

Mamta shouts at him, 'Motherfucker.'

FASIL ROAD STARTS at the Ajmeri Gate intersection. Facing the gateway is a Bosch showroom, fronted by dark glass panels. The corridor that separates GB Road from Fasil Road begins with Sir Sobha Singh Building. Sobha Singh, the father of author Khushwant Singh, was one of the principal building contractors of British-built New Delhi.

The paved lobby-like space has men sleeping on the doorsteps of the shuttered shops. A brand new tonga is resting against a wall. Nearby, a paan vendor is loudly talking to his customers, telling them about the mysterious disappearance of a relative.

I continue walking.

Both sides are lined with shops selling machine spare parts, toilet seats and motor pumps. The shops on the left are actually the establishments that are on GB Road. These are their back entrances. A young woman in a pink sari and loose hair walks past me, her anklets making a *chham-chhua* sound. A boy with a Christ tattoo on his arm looks her straight in the eye as she passes him by.

Though it is noon, it is all shadows, as if the sun never enters the lane.

I turn back and see Ajmeri Gate; it is bathed in sunlight. Behind it, the glass high-rise of the Municipal Corporation of Delhi.

Ahead of me, down the lane, two men are inhaling heroin fumes from a heated aluminium foil. Beside them is a snack vendor. A woman in a black burka buys 5 rupees worth of peanuts from him.

I stop by Premier Engineering Works—a little shop. 'We supply motor generator sets to engineering colleges where they are used by students for training purposes,' says Javed Manzoor Sheikh, whose father founded the store in the 1960s. 'We live close by, in Daryaganj.'

Pointing to the back windows of the kothas, I ask, 'Have you any idea of the women there?'

'No,' he says. 'The market closes by seven and then we go home. I don't know what happens here after that. Men who work here never go up to the kothas. Those are for outsiders. We actually want this to end. The kothas are not a good thing for this area. I rarely see the women coming this side. If they want juice or fruits, there are vendors who go up to give it to them. Sometimes, actually, they do come down when they want recharge coupons for their mobile phones. It's always older women who come. The younger women live like queens. When they grow old, they don't get customers and then, I think, they have to run errands for the younger lot.'

Javed takes me to a friend who runs a mobile phone kiosk in the lane. Muhammed Sahil is getting ready for his marriage next week. After patiently listening to me, he playfully rubs his crotch and laughs, saying, 'Don't hang out in GB Road, brother. Very dangerous place. Everyone who comes here returns crying.'

We laugh.

After I prod him further, he says, 'Yes, women come to me from upstairs to get recharge cards. On some days, I see ten. But there are also days when I see no woman from the kothas. Everyone, without exception, calls me brother. They talk very politely to me. Here they act like any ordinary woman. Their bodies are covered, and you can't make out that they are prostitutes.

'Some of them are very poor and I have to recharge their mobile phones on credit. But I've no hesitation doing that. These women are very honest. They always pay up what they owe me, which could be this evening, tomorrow, next week or next month. They never cheat.'

We are joined by another friend of Javed. His shirt buttons are open and his hairy chest shows a silver ring hanging from a thick black thread.

'This street changes colour after 10 p.m.,' says Sahil. 'Don't try coming here at that hour. The place is invaded by addicts. They don't differentiate between a man and an animal. They would knife you for your cash, mobile or watch, anything that could get them their smack.'

As I walk out of the kiosk, the man with the hairy chest speaks out in a sing-song voice as if he is reciting a couplet:

Duniya khatam ho jayegi
Chudhai nahin hogi
(The world might end,
But not the fucking)

THE WOMEN IN NUMBER 300 have no need to step out of the kotha. Vendors come to them, selling toffee, honey, nail polish. One afternoon, I climb the stairs with a masseur, who has mustard oil bottles in his bag. 'I massage the joints of the women. The pain disappears instantly,' he mutters.

In winter, young Kashmiri men who drive buses in the valley escape the snow-blocked region and live for a few months in Delhi, where they sell woollen clothes. They, too, come to GB Road. This evening, Mahesh Kumar, a seller of plastic necklaces and anklets, is sitting in the courtyard. Phalak has chosen one pendant. She goes inside to get the money, leaving me with Kumar. He tells me, 'You look like an educated man.'

'You look decent, too,' I say.

Nighat walks in from the kitchen. 'Will you have chai?' she asks Kumar.

He smiles in gratitude and gently shakes his head. Nighat leaves for the balcony.

Leaning close to me, Kumar says, 'These women . . . I don't think they bathe after doing it with the customer.'

'You could be right,' I say.

'Very dirty,' he shakes his head, making a face as if he has tasted something bitter.

WHEN SUSHMA NEEDS TO BUY VEGETABLES, or Phalak wants better-quality cardigans and shawls than what the Kashmiris sell, they go to Sitaram Bazaar.

Bazaars like Chandni Chowk and Karol Bagh are visited only to buy clothes for special occasions; most women in GB Road do their ordinary shopping—daily wear, spices, vegetables, kitchen utensils—in Sitaram Bazaar.

The market is on the other side of Ajmeri Gate; follow the road that heads to Chawri Bazaar and walk into the first turning on the right. The alley turns and twists and ends up in Sitaram Bazaar. I want to take in the sights and sounds experienced by the women in the kothas by tracing their route to the bazaar.

The lane off the road to Chawri Bazaar opens in an unsettling manner. A chhole–kulche vendor stands right opposite a men's urinal. The principal sight at the next turning is a giant banyan tree growing out of a wall. A brass bell hangs from one of its branches. Its trunk is smeared with saffron paste. It is a temple.

This is a quiet lane. Married women, with red sindoor in the parting of their hair, walk holding the hands of their children. Old houses stand on both sides; some are locked, their windows broken and balconies cracked. Calendars of previous years—they have no use now—are plastered on the walls of these closed houses. Since they carry pictures of gods, they cannot be thrown away.

I pass a tailoring shop. Somewhere a Hindi film song is playing. Soon I reach a haveli called Prakash Bhawan. It is newly painted. I sit on its front steps, imagining Phalak walking past with Imran in her arms.

A woman is walking alone. Her eyes are cast down; her head is covered with the free end of her sari.

Now, I'm in Sitaram Bazaar. Vegetable stalls, groceries, a kiosk to repair watches, a few shops selling clothes, a toy store. Once, Phalak had bought a police officer's uniform for Imran from here.

While walking back, I stop by a haveli. A woman in a sari sits in the courtyard, picking rice from a thali. The door is open, and the woman seems to be alone. I wonder if her husband is at work, and if her children are at school. Is she preparing lunch for them?

Have Phalak or Sushma or Mamta or Roopa or Sumaira ever chanced upon this woman while on their way to Sitaram Bazaar? What would they make of her life?

ELECTRIC CABLES. Machine-part shops. This is so similar to GB Road. But GB Road does not have the graceful Mubarak Begum mosque.

Situated in the congested Lal Kuan, the bazaar across Farash Khana, the mosque is on top of the shops. The pale-green entrance door is tucked between two stores selling bolts, cables and welding rod electrodes. A flight of steep stairs leads to a courtyard, the sudden openness of which comes as a surprise.

The courtyard has an ablution tank and two large pots planted with vines. The centrepiece is the mosque, in red sandstone. It is painted a shade of brick dust. Its three entrance arches correspond to its three domes; the central arch and dome are the largest of the three. Two rotating fans are mounted on both sides of the central doorway. A cat is balanced on the parapet.

Built in the early nineteenth century, the mosque was named after one of the thirteen wives of David Ochterlony, Delhi's first British resident, who was known for his passion for nautch girls, hookahs and Indian costumes. Mubarak Begum, a Brahmin dancing girl from Pune, was a convert to Islam. Besides being Ochterlony's favourite wife (some say she was just a mistress), she was a principal player in Delhi's cultural life. One of Delhi's last great mushairas or poetry soirees was said to have been hosted in her haveli just before the Mughal empire came to an end. Forty poets were present that night, including Mirza Ghalib.

It is not clear if the mosque was commissioned by Mubarak Begum or was built in her honour. It is crudely nicknamed *Randi ki Masjid* after one of the Urdu words for prostitute. The moniker may have come from her perceived mistress status.

The dark prayer chamber inside the mosque cannot accommodate more than ten men. Its homely smallness emphasizes the theatricality of the huge domes. The floor is marble, the walls are painted pale yellow and the Mecca-facing mihrab is in glossy green. The noise from outside—the honking of the scooters—is subdued.

A few steps away is the Chawri Bazaar metro station. Years ago, the dancing women were removed from the Chawri market and shifted to GB Road, across the Old Delhi wall, just beyond the city's boundary. But this Randi ki Masjid, or the mosque of the whore, remains within the city.

Watching the mosque from across the street gives one a fairytale feeling. Perhaps it is because the area is so ordinary and lacking in any character that the domes seem infused with a special rounded sweetness. Stare longer and the disagreeable aesthetics of the modern world dampens the mosque's delicate beauty. It is looking at something—perhaps a way of life—that seems to have already disappeared.

Nobody can love you more than me

Nighat Khala has left.

'She left last night by Karnataka Express,' Omar says. 'She has gone to our grandmother's house in Bangalore. She might not return. It happened suddenly.'

Sabir Bhai is sleeping; so is Phalak. I go to Fatima.

'I don't know. Nothing happened,' she says.

Omar shakes his head. 'Yes, nothing happened. She just left.'

Nighat has been in number 300 from the time before Omar was born. The children have grown up under her care. During the day, she sat on the veranda, waiting for customers. She called Masoom a piece of her heart, *jigar ka tukda*. Every afternoon, she combed her long hair while standing on the balcony, looking at the street below. Her face was very expressive until she put on make-up. She had a room upstairs to entertain customers. I have never seen it.

Once, sitting on the bench, she had casually hitched up her salwar, giving me a glimpse of her hairy legs.

A few days later, Omar tells me the reason for Nighat Khala's abrupt exit.

She could not have done it. Perhaps Sabir Bhai is mistaken. In any case, I do not wish to disclose it in this book. Khala's reputation must not be compromised. The reader does not need to know everything.

213

IN THESE THREE YEARS in GB Road, have I recorded the truth?

What if Sushma never met the man whom she says she loved and who died falling from a roof? What if her friend Chhovi was a fabrication? What if Roopa's story about her husband is a lie? What if Sabir Bhai is not what he seems to be?

MAYBE IT IS BETTER THIS WAY. It is fulfilling enough for a writer to get a sense of GB Road without stripping bare the lives of its people.

Sabir Bhai believes that long after my book is published, I will still be thinking of Omar, Osman, Masoom and Imran. He believes I will visit them as always.

DIVYA BHARTI IS BITING HER NAILS. Bipasha Basu's spaghetti straps fall off her shoulders. Rani Mukherjee is posing with a sunflower. Aishwarya Rai is cycling in a garden of pink tulips. Aamir Khan is kissing Kajol.

Nighat Khala's chamber where she entertained customers is crowded with the posters of film stars. Omar is showing them to me. The room is clean. I lie down on the bed. The roof has brass-coloured tiles. A tube light glows white. The small side table has an empty mineral water bottle, a glass, an empty packet of Haldiram namkeen and an old issue of *India Today* magazine. A ledge on the wall has a soap case and a box of condoms. The box shows a man and a woman looking at each other, not caring for the setting sun (or is it rising?). It says:

DELUXE NIRODH

FOR FAMILY PLANNING

'We pleaded with Khala not to go,' Omar says. 'She was crying.'

Something is scrawled in blue ink on a poster that shows a lake with two swans:

Nighat—I love u,
Nobody can love u more than me
Thanks. Manoj—21/12/2010

'He is Khala's friend. He lives in Dubai and visits us about three times a year. Last time, he took us on a full day's outing to Connaught Place. McDonald's was crowded, so we got the burgers packed and ate them in Central Park. Then we went to Palika Bazaar, where he bought a video game for Masoom. He got a black leather overcoat for Khala, like the one Rani Mukherjee is wearing in this poster.'

'Will Khala come back?' I ask.

'I think she will.'

'OSMAN, COVER THE GOAT WITH HIS SACK. It's almost evening,' Sabir Bhai says. He is warming his hands over a small wood-fired stove. The goat is the latest member of the household. It is to be cared for until next year when it will be sacrificed on Eid. 'We have named him Salman,' Osman says. Imran is running in slow motion like a movie star in the final scene of an action film. He has a green plastic revolver with which he pretends to shoot us.

'The day Allah decides that our time is over in GB Road, we will leave this kotha,' Sabir Bhai says. 'All of us are destined to live in the places where we live. Your fate is to write. Mine is to make a living in this area. I surely do not want to breathe my last here. Dying in GB Road is not good . . . '

Picking up from where Sabir Bhai tapers off, Phalak, who is chopping spinach, says, 'If a Muslim dies in a red light area, it is difficult to get a maulana for his funeral procession.'

215

'The only thing I can tell you is that I'm not from this world,' Sabir Bhai says. 'I was born in Kanpur. I spent my childhood in a relative's house. But if you want to know how I came to Delhi, how I started living here . . . there are many reasons why people are forced to leave the land of their fathers . . . but I don't want to share it.'

I follow Sabir Bhai into his room where he takes out a file from a bedside shelf. Showing me his newspaper cuttings—hundreds of them—Sabir Bhai says, 'I have been collecting these for years.'

Four Uzbek call girls held in Lajpat Nagar

Spa employee raped in Dwarka

Sex racket: Russian, 3 others held

Life term for rape of epileptic girl

Manipur girl raped after given a lift in Delhi

Neighbour raped teen for 3 days

High-profile sex racket busted in East Delhi

'Do you see how much dirt there is in society?' Sabir Bhai says. 'I want to tell the world that the world outside GB Road is filthier. Imagine how much worse the situation would be if there were no red light areas.

'I pray to Allah that you make your name with your book, but I too intend to write a book on GB Road. I have seen so much here, experienced so many things; I have observed from close range the lives of the women here . . . I know their problems, I know why and how most of them come here. It would all go into my book. I hope that one day that book will be made into a film or a TV series. Then more people would be able to understand our life in GB Road. Right now, society only thinks that we are dirty and that we bring women here by force or by duping them.'

'Sabir Bhai has taken the children to Kalyar Sharif,' Phalak says, referring to a Sufi shrine about a hundred miles from Delhi.

She is in the kitchen, heating mustard oil in a pan. Imran hasn't accompanied his brothers. He is eating a samosa on the veranda. 'Fatima went along, too. They will be back in a week.'

Phalak throws chopped tomatoes into the pan. 'He goes there every year. He is a very good Muslim and this is something about his character that has not changed since I first knew him. I met him seventeen or eighteen or twenty years ago when I first arrived in GB Road with my friends from Bangalore. He was then in 156, doing the same thing there. Initially, since it was a new place and I was a new arrival, I was not sure what kind of a man he was. But, I think, he has remained the same person. At that time, he did not talk about politics as he does now. He was also more charitable. In winters, he gifted blankets to beggars in Jama Masjid.'

Phalak covers the pan with a lid and goes to the veranda. Sitting on the bench, she starts breastfeeding Imran.

'Then, as now, his earnings came from the women who lived in his kotha. He has always taken good care of them. He got them new clothes on festivals. Every Friday, after returning from his afternoon prayers in Jama Masjid, he gave 100 rupees to each woman. He was addicted to charas so we called him Charsi.'

Remembering that Fatima had once expressed bitter feelings towards Sabir Bhai, I ask, 'What does Fatima think about him?'

Phalak says, 'How can I speak for what goes on in her heart?'

Imran turns away from Phalak's breast and stares at the balcony.

'Sabir never used to lose his temper. Today he is less calm. I started respecting him after Omar was born. We have been living together ever since. Now I'm forty, forty-four, and a mother of four children. I have accepted him in my heart. What is the need for a marriage?'

WHEN I FIRST SAW IMRAN about three years ago, he could only crawl on the floor. Now he runs menacingly like a Bollywood hero in search of villains. Masoom has grown fatter. Omar and Osman remain bony. Omar has grown more religious.

EACH TIME I SEE MAMTA climbing the stairs with a customer, I feel happy. There will be money. Mamta will be able to buy more red tank tops and plastic heels from Chandni Chowk. Sabir Bhai will get his commission. The children's fees will be paid. There will be meat more often for dinner. Who knows what tomorrow will be like? Maybe one of the sons will go to college and become an engineer. He might get a good job in a multinational company. Sabir Bhai might move the family out of GB Road. But what about Mamta? Suppose she earns so much money that she never ever has to work again, what would she like to do? I go down to the arcade where she is calling out to men and ask her.

'Hello Soofi, why are you getting so thin? Why don't you eat?' Mamta clings to me. I feel her breast against me. Taking me inside, to the stairwell, she says, 'Go back, people will see you. Talk to Sabir Bhai. I will get you omelette–toast.' Mamta's reply to my query is incoherent. She laughs and requests me again to go back to Sabir Bhai while she gets toast for me.

To her, perhaps, my question is too outlandish to merit a reply.

WE ARE REACHING the end of November. It is getting colder. A South African friend in Jor Bagh who knows that I go to GB Road daily has given me her cashmere shawl, asking me to present it to any woman in need. The shawl is light blue and extremely soft. Feeling it on my cheek, I'm tempted to keep it for myself. I will give it to Mamta.

'Soofi, is this for me?' Phalak says, pointing to the shawl I have wrapped in today's newspaper. Taking it from me, Fatima says, 'Give it to me, Soofi. I'm very cold and I don't have a warm cardigan.'

I take it back from her. Mamta is not around. 'The shawl is for me,' I say in irritation.

THE MARBLE FLOOR IS ICY. It is about midnight and I'm in Hazrat Nizamuddin Dargah. The Sufi saint's grave-chamber is closed, and the courtyard is empty but for a partially paralysed old man who is bowing his head on the floor. I have seen him begging during the day. He is shivering. I drape the cashmere shawl around his shoulders.

I TAKE SUSHMA'S HANDS in mine. It is a few minutes to midnight. The New Year countdown has begun. Sushma is dancing with me to the film song '*Chhammak chhallo*'. I'm Shah Rukh Khan, she is Kareena Kapoor.

Holding my forefinger over her head, she twirls. I take both her arms and together we turn around. We repeat the steps. Sushma laughs and hides her face in my chest. Meanwhile, Imran is shooting at us with his plastic revolver. Omar is making a video of us on his Chinese mobile phone. Sitting on the bench, Phalak is clapping. Sabir Bhai is watching TV news in his room. Osman, the disc jockey for the night, is manning the stereo. Suddenly, Masoom cries out and starts spraying us with artificial snow. 'Happy New Year!' he shouts.

Sabir Bhai appears, greeting us. Sushma runs to the latrine, laughing hysterically.

Osman starts a new song. Sushma comes back. Now, I'm Salman Khan and she is Katrina Kaif.

Acknowledgements

Gaurav Sood, for constantly nudging me to write

Ranjana Sengupta, who first had the idea and believed in the second edition

Sanchita Guha, the first reader of every chapter

Marina Bang, the dearest, who designed this book

Anna Gerotto for loving my work enough to help me see it with new eyes

Dayanita Singh, Diane Raines Ward and Priya Ramani for inspiration

Roger Choate, Steven Baker and Nipa Charagi for helping me shape my writing

Sukumar Ranganathan, editor, *Hindustan Times*, for trusting me with my dream job

Kunal Pradhan for being the boss others can't even dream of

Sadia Dehlvi for food and love, Rakhshanda Jalil for gossip, Aanchal Malhotra for something profound but difficult to pinpoint, and Elena Tommaseo for her generous heart (and never-enough bathua risotto)

Raluca Sidon, Adil Bhoja, Namya Sinha and Abhinav Bamhi for their friendship

William Shakespeare, Jane Austen, Emily Dickinson, Marcel Proust and Arundhati Roy for lighting up my world

Jonas Moses-Lustiger, for being there with me in the final scene of this book